The Unofficial Guide to
ADOPTIVE PARENTING

by the same author

No Matter What
An Adoptive Family's Story of Hope, Love and Healing
Sally Donovan
ISBN 978 1 84905 431 7
eISBN 978 0 85700 781 0

of related interest

Why Can't My Child Behave?
Empathic Parenting Strategies that Work for Adoptive and Foster Families
Dr Amber Elliott
ISBN 978 1 84905 339 6
eISBN 978 0 85700 671 4

Attaching in Adoption
Practical Tools for Today's Parents
Deborah D. Gray
ISBN 978 1 84905 890 2
eISBN 978 0 85700 606 6

Attaching Through Love, Hugs and Play
Simple Strategies to Help Build Connections with Your Child
Deborah D. Gray
ISBN 978 1 84905 939 8
eISBN 978 0 85700 753 7

Attachment in Common Sense and Doodles
A Practical Guide
Miriam Silver
ISBN 978 1 84905 314 3
eISBN 978 0 85700 624 0

Adopted Like Me
My Book of Adopted Heroes
Ann Angel
ISBN 978 1 84905 935 0
eISBN 978 0 85700 740 7

Can I tell you about Adoption?
A guide for friends, family and professionals
Anne Braff Brodzinsky
ISBN 978 1 84905 942 8
eISBN 978 0 85700 759 9

The Unofficial Guide to

ADOPTIVE PARENTING

The Small Stuff, The Big Stuff
and The Stuff In Between

SALLY DONOVAN

Forewords by Vivien Norris
and Jim Clifford OBE and Sue Clifford

Jessica Kingsley *Publishers*
London and Philadelphia

First published in 2015
by Jessica Kingsley Publishers
73 Collier Street
London N1 9BE, UK
and
400 Market Street, Suite 400
Philadelphia, PA 19106, USA

www.jkp.com

Library of Congress Cataloging in Publication Data
Donovan, Sally (Adoptive mother)
  No matter what : an adoptive family's story of hope, love and healing / Sally Donovan.
    pages cm
  ISBN 978-1-84905-431-7 (alk. paper)
  1. Donovan, Sally (Adoptive mother) 2. Adoptive parents--Great Britain--Biography. 3.
Abused children--Great Britain--Biography. 4. Adoption--Great Britain. I. Title.
  HV874.82.D66A3 2013
  362.734092'2--dc23

                          2013005856

British Library Cataloguing in Publication Data
A CIP catalogue record for this book is available from the British Library

ISBN 978 1 84905 536 9
eISBN 978 0 85700 959 3

Printed and bound in Great Britain

CONTENTS

ACKNOWLEDGEMENTS

There are so many people to thank. First off, because I have no idea how I'd have survived the last few years without him, and because unforgivably I forgot to thank him in my first book *No Matter What*, I must say to Mr D., thank you for keeping me sane, for loving me and for allowing me to share our lives with other adopters. I love you very much.

Thank you to our children for teaching me so much about trauma particularly through your beautiful drawings and incredible writing and for keeping on when I was at times a bit slow on the uptake. I love you both very much and I'm sorry I just can't marry you.

Thank you to the professionals, Mrs M. and Mr R. in particular who have taught me most of this and whom I wish I could name here.

Thank you to all the adopters and adoptees I have great pleasure to meet and talk to both face-to-face and on social media. I continue to learn lots from you.

Thank you to Amanda. You are one of the most remarkable 'robins' I've met. Your encouragement and your insistence that I delete the 'very's has been a massive help. And thanks to the rest of the Whitby gang too. Turning a mind-blowing awful situation into something so positive is nothing short of heroic.

Thank you to my parents for continuing to support us and to my sister and her family for great kindness.

Thank you to Fran Proctor and S. for sharing your experiences and learning with me so generously.

And finally thank you to Stephen and everyone at Jessica Kingsley Publishers for your encouragement and help.

To the Winner of all books

FOREWORD

There is a big difference between understanding what a traumatised child has suffered and may need, and the reality of attempting to provide therapeutic parenting in practice. In this new book Sally Donovan communicates powerfully the messy lived experience of daily family life with her two adopted children; in turns confusing, infuriating, exhausting, wonderful, frightening, lonely and precious. Like many adoptive parents, Sally has had a mixed experience of both professional and personal support and has often had to weather the lack of understanding of her situation. She has had to sift through conflicting guidance to find pragmatic approaches for managing the day-to-day manifestations of trauma expressed by her children. The intensity of the parenting challenges is often hard for parents of non-traumatised children to grasp, but fellow adoptive parents and their supporters will instantly recognise what she is talking about. And in her hopeful, intelligent, moving, witty and psychologically sound reflections they will gain a lot of comfort.

There is of course much more we could and should be doing to provide useful support to adoptive families and a growing body of approaches to draw from. It is essential that we listen to the experiences of adoptive parents; about what is humanly possible and what is not, about what works in practice and what makes things much worse; and importantly to face thinking about some of the often unspoken challenges that adoptive parents may be facing alone. This book will be an invaluable resource for both parents, extended family and friends, and professionals.

Dr Vivien Norris

Consultant Clinical Psychologist, DDP Practitioner, Certified Theraplay® Therapist and Trainer, The Family Place

FOREWORD

Like Sally, we adopted children because we wanted to be parents, and that has proved such a glorious, and a gloriously trying, experience. Over the years we have learned how much these adopted children, as well as many who aren't, need a different sort of parenting. Love and acceptance go hand in hand, but for these children, that acceptance must also embrace and live with their trauma, their developmental gaps, their world view which screams danger at every turn, and their huge challenges in forming effective attachments. We need to reach into their worlds and hold their hands as we come out together. Perhaps the biggest challenge is to do this whilst retaining some semblance of 'normal' family life: but it is possible.

We have spoken to many adoptive parents recently who have been trained in the theory of therapeutic parenting and parenting with PLACE (playfulness, love, acceptance, curiosity and empathy). They have also been trained to understand their child's pathology, how early life experiences of abuse, neglect and loss have impacted on their brain development and current behaviours. What seems to be lacking is, in practical terms, how to apply the theory. Over and over again we have heard adopters say 'I understand the effect on my child – but tell me how to parent them. What does this sort of parenting look like?'

In her book Sally tells us what it looks like. Through her accounts of what has and hasn't worked for her family she offers practical advice on how to apply the theory. She is refreshingly honest, giving us permission, not only to parent differently, but also to make mistakes and to be human. As successful adopters of nine traumatised children, this book resonates so well with our own experience. Each child is different, so what works for one may not work for another. Over the last 24 years we have used most of the techniques employed by Sally, and we have encountered many of the challenges experienced by her and her family.

Sally's ideas don't form a prescriptive methodology. This is not a formula that you can get 'right' or 'wrong'. Some of them (and there are plenty) will suit some families and some won't. What will fit, though, is her mixture of honesty, humour and love, and her encouragement to balance understanding for the child with trying not to make it too hard on yourself as a parent.

If we had had this book to refer to many years ago it would have helped us to parent our children more easily. It is not a text book and it is not prescriptive. It is a practical guide, easy to read, full of helpful advice and strategies to try for children where traditional parenting methods fail because our children have not had a traditional childhood experience. It is a must read for all adoptive parents.

Read it, get ideas from it, but above all smile at it, and use it to help you smile again with your family.

Jim Clifford OBE and Sue Clifford[1]

---

1   Sue and Jim have adopted nine of the most traumatised children over the last 24 years. The story of their youngest was told in Jacci Parry's highly-acclaimed BBC2 documentary 'A Home for Maisie'. Sue is a well-known speaker, author and trainer on therapeutic parenting. Inspired by their experiences, Jim led the development in 2013 of 'It's All About Me', the National Adoption Bond that finds, trains and supports families for Harder to Place children. He received an OBE in 2013 for this, and his wider work in social impact and social investment.

INTRODUCTION

Eleven years ago and after a restless night spent listening to the church bells ringing out into the small hours, my husband Mr D. and I got into our car and returned two-and-a-half hours later with our two children, then aged one and four years old. We had first met them two weeks before. Even now, after all we have experienced together, the bizarreness of that day still strikes me. There are days that change one's life momentously and forever and that day was certainly one of them.

I wrote about the experience of adopting Jamie and Rose in my first book *No Matter What*. It was borne out of a need to record what felt like a very different and more intense family life to those being lived around me. At the time I started writing I thought our experiences must be quite uncommon, but as I started blogging and connecting with others on social media, and then when *No Matter What* hit the shops, the response from readers demonstrated that many adopters were facing a very similar set of challenges. The overwhelming feedback has been, 'Thank you for writing this, it's as though you have understood and written about *my* life.' It has not only been read by adopters and prospective adopters but also by extended family members who report that reading the book has helped them to connect with what their nearest and dearest are going through, and to understand what they most need in terms of support. Being in the thick of adoptive parenting can be gruelling and emotionally taxing and we can find ourselves lost for words. It was important to me to get across what this feels like because we can so easily be misunderstood, and worse still, blamed for the difficulties we experience.

Parenting children who have known the worst of times is different from average, everyday parenting no matter how hard we may try to convince ourselves otherwise. Traditional parenting styles and expectations and measures of success just don't cut it in a family that has been stitched together as a result of loss and often trauma and neglect as well. The pervasive and persuasive myth that a child's past can be washed away by the act of adoption, a hearty routine and plenty of love falls apart for many of us very early on. The debunking of that myth is well overdue and has to be replaced with clear and unwavering honesty; honesty about the impact upon children of loss and trauma and honesty about the therapeutic approaches which help them to gain a sense of safety, security, self-worth and belonging.

Over the past 11 years I have been on courses, attended conferences, read books, watched DVDs, listened to CDs and met with social workers in an effort to understand the approaches which work when nothing else does. All of that learning has been invaluable and I still pursue it; in fact I don't think will ever stop learning. The challenge I've found though is not necessarily in the learning but in the application of the learning. There is, in our house at least, a reality gap between all the good, clean therapeutic methods and the day-in day-out, multi-dimensional, messy, dynamic, domestic landscape which we inhabit. On top of that I am the parent of siblings which adds a great level of complexity to the parenting equation. And on top of that I am an imperfect human being. I make mistakes. All the time. It took me ages to realise that that was all right and to stop blaming myself.

In this book, my second, I have gathered together everything I've learnt and tested and amended and retested and found to be practical and effective. I've shared the mistakes as well as the triumphs, and covered everything from the everyday routines like getting up in the morning and mealtimes to difficult and challenging behaviours like anger and swearing. I have found myself questioning some well-accepted subjects such as 'life story work' and tackling some taboo ones too, such as violence between siblings. I have worked hard not to avoid any difficult topics and to at all times apply the honesty test.

Whether you've come to this *Unofficial Guide* as an adoptive or prospective adoptive parent or as someone supporting a family, I hope you find it useful, readable and practical. Don't expect reverent, rose-tinted or worthy because that's not my bag. I also don't do preachy or simplistic. Therapeutic, adoptive parenting is a demanding and imperfect discipline, but there is one thing I am certain of: it enables families to create the conditions for acceptance, nurture, growth and rich experience which can bring about the most profound breakthroughs in our children's lives.

CHAPTER 1

IT'S ALL ABOUT US – SHAPING UP TO BE A THERAPEUTIC PARENT

Unpicking our parenting

'Beauty is in the eye of the beholder,' said someone. What they didn't say was, 'I'm going to fix you until I find you beautiful.' I'm starting here, with us, the beholders of our children, because so much of therapeutic parenting is not about our children at all, but about us.

Twelve years ago I went to an 'adoption preparation' session in an airless local authority conference room and listened to a social worker talking about how we must reflect upon how we were parented, in order that we may become the parents our future children need. I thought I had done all the reflecting and that was that, job done and box ticked, and I didn't give it much more thought. Now, 12 years later, I have had to completely deconstruct not only how I was parented, but how my parents were parented, how their parents were parented and how just about everyone I know was parented. I even find myself thinking about how major historical figures were parented. Would Kaiser Wilhelm II have marched quite so enthusiastically into the First World War had his parents not treated him so harshly I wonder? Barely a Channel 4 history documentary goes by without there being some terrible and damaging parenting lurking somewhere in the nursery.

The way I was parented has snuck into my brain like a line of viral computer code, and before I remodelled myself as a therapeutic parent I had almost no control over how and when it would show itself. I want to stress that I was parented well and it has stood *me* well. My childhood was classic 1970s: strict in some ways (never leave any food on the plate, never answer back ever, be naughty get sent to your room) and in other ways quite *laissez-faire* (here's a jam sandwich and a Wagon Wheel, now go out and play in the woods for the day).

If you know anything about therapeutic parenting then you will have already spotted my weak points. My methods of parenting, which I had unconsciously inherited from my parents (which they had unconsciously inherited from theirs) collapsed into total inadequacy very soon after I was told to 'Get lost, fat loser.' I've since heard much worse, and believe me a lecture and a sending to bed will get you nowhere fast. So too will 'How dare you speak to me like that' or its close cousin, 'I would never have spoken to my parents like that.' (And so too will sticker charts and magic beads, but that post-dates my childhood, so more about that later.)

Some of us go in the other direction and react against the way we were parented, for good reason perhaps. We must still guard against this. Adopted children need to be parented in a manner which takes full account of *their* past experiences, not ours.

Instead of allowing our parenting to tumble unthinkingly out of our mouths, as therapeutic parents we have no choice but to get educated, learn new methods, forgive ourselves for our mistakes and gradually rebuild ourselves in the new model. For me it's been an ongoing process and I am much-improved, but still a bit rough around the edges: a project under-completion. That might be the best it ever gets.

You might be feeling heat rising from your belly as you read this: 'The issue here is not MY parenting,' you might be thinking, 'it's my CHILDREN who are the problem.' If you are, and I don't seek to blame you at all for that, then I respectfully suggest you read on. When something associated around therapeutic parenting makes us feel angry and dogmatic, in my experience that's a big clue that we have hit a sizeable, emotional roadblock.

Good grief, is that a roadblock?

Adoption is life-changing and life-affirming *and* it has come about through loss. Loss and grief can hang around a family home like an unwelcome and unwashed guest at a party, stoking resentment, bitterness and anger. They refuse to move on until looked at full in the face and touched and accepted with courage. Having suffered monumental loss (so much has been taken from them), our children need adults around them strong enough to accept and to some extent hold that loss and grief with them. To be up to that job we have to acknowledge and process our own grief first.

Grief is not commonly associated with what never was, but rather with what was and is no more. Many of us come to adoption via undesired childlessness. We may have anticipated raising biological children, who look a bit like us, sound like us, have some of our traits and talents and who fit neatly into our family trees. They can almost exist, in a ghostly way, and yet they will never make it across the ether into reality. We have to let go of the hope of ever meeting them and that is itself a loss. To really throw open our arms to a ready-made, probably damaged and grieving adopted child can only be done with gusto and meaning once we have really faced and addressed our own ghostly grief. Although mine left the party a long time ago, it occasionally makes a surprise reappearance, but it is familiar now, passes quickly and serves as a useful reminder of the grief our children feel.

It is important I think to process grief, particularly that associated with childlessness, before we embark on adoption and therapeutic parenting. I have been party to conversations about the wisdom or otherwise of starting the adoption process within weeks of a failed IVF cycle, or indeed even if IVF and adoption should be pursued in parallel. I get that strong desire to be a parent, I really do, but I don't recommend rushing into adoption as an insurance policy, a second-best. Adopted children need to be first choice, best, most-wanted, someone's number one.

Tempting though it is to fit the blinkers, lock grief away in a secret drawer and pretend it doesn't exist, it won't stay locked away for long and when it breaks free it may wash over our families in a tidal wave. When we are the rock that our children are clinging to, it's not just our own emotional health which is at risk.

I am not a grief counsellor or a psychologist, but I can speak from experience. I would say be brave, confront grief and don't feel ashamed of how it makes you feel. And give yourself time. Don't make yourself feel like an utter shit when your first gut feeling on hearing that someone you know is pregnant is jealous disappointment. Talk to friends and family members who understand (don't talk to ANYONE who doesn't understand, it will make you want to hurt them). Grief is not polite, nor is it pretty, and it gets you when you're down. Locking it up isn't going to make it go away.

Great expectations

We all have hopes and dreams for our children. We may want them to be good at sport, because we are, or achieve academically, because we did or because we didn't. We may want them to be popular because that's something we see as important, to join lots of clubs and have lots of friends. Whatever it is, we all think we know what makes a good human being. Looking back, I was particularly rigid in my thinking. My children were going to be well-read, sociable, do their homework and enjoy learning, because that's what I'm like. I was expecting to parent a mini-me. How vain is that?

It may sound ridiculous to talk again about grief here, but there is a letting go to be done. Letting go of our expectations, hopes, dreams, whatever they are, allows the process of acceptance to take place. Our children become part of our families with their own personalities and strengths and possibilities, and we must not allow our own hopes to prevent us from seeing, accepting and nurturing theirs. Their strengths and interests may lead us in directions we had never imagined and teach us things we never would have learnt. I'm not saying we shouldn't be ambitious for them, but it's different from being ambitious for ourselves.

One small example. I've never been 'an animal person' because my parents weren't (how daft is that?). I now share my life with a cat, two guinea pigs and six fish and have cause to stroke several horses on a regular basis. Not life-changing on a grand scale, but the relationship I have with Ron the Cat has in a small but not insignificant way changed my life for the better. The only reason I know the joy of Ron the Cat is my animal-mad and wonderful daughter.

Value-ables

I've come to learn that my values are different from my dreams. My values are hard and have meaning whereas my dreams are flimsy vanity projects like my pretend mini-me children. My values might be similar to yours and are about how we should treat other people, how we should approach work and money and how we present ourselves to the outside world. There was a time when I felt my values were being trampled on and would be lost forever (another victim of past abuse and neglect). I've realised (with help) that my values are what makes me, me and though I may be prepared to compromise around the edges of them, they are a stake in the ground. If I give up on them I might as well throw in the towel.

Non-single adopters will almost certainly have to negotiate competing values. Some aspects of parenting traumatised children are more challenging as a couple than as a single person (easy for me to say as one of a couple), and this is one of them. Our values may look ridiculous to our partner and theirs to us and adoptive parenting shines a great big light on these differences, which we may have worked hard at ignoring up until now. Our values have to be treated with respect. But each must be looked at with honesty. Some 'values' are merely dreams and expectations dressed up a bit. Sometimes I think that the process of parenting traumatised children is one continuous test of what is and isn't important. Believe me, there are loads of things we think of as important which are not.

The brittle voice

It is tempting to want a broken child fixed, so we can get on with our lives, just as we are. It is tempting to be rigid and uncompromising and say things like, 'If I tell you to do that, you do it' and, 'What I say goes.' It is tempting also to go on courses and sit cross-armed huffing and puffing about how we know all the brain stuff; we just want to be told how to make our child behave normally. It is tempting to think that all our child needs is firmer discipline, stronger boundaries and some straight talking. It is tempting to respond to every piece of advice with, 'Yeah but…' before boring the room about how despicable our child is. Frankly it is tempting to spend a lot of time in transmit mode.

Transmit mode is where we are in danger of going when we are exhausted and scared and clinging on to our broken parenting methods for grim death. It may be that that's our parenting style of last resort out of desperation or because we are lapsing back into the parenting styles of our parents. In order to be effective therapeutic parents we must spend most of our time in receive and learn mode. I'm sorry if that's not what you wanted to hear.

Deep inside our children, hidden beneath the rage and the anxiety, the scabs and the scars, is a brittle voice which has been silenced by fear and shame. If we learn how to listen, the brittle voice tells of how the world is to our child. Many aspects of their behaviour are fuelled by the brittle voice as their behaviour is the only way they know of communicating with us. As they get older, feel a little safer and start to make sense of their past experiences you may hear their voice in a form you are more familiar with. And then you will be hit with what they have carried with them all along: I am bad, I am worthless, I am unlovable, sooner or later I will be rejected again, everything bad that has happened to me was my fault. You may get to hear their deepest fears: I worry every day that I will be snatched off the street, I worry someone will take me from my bed, I worry I will lose you and never see you again. These are not passing fears and beliefs – the brittle voice is like a motor which drives how our children perceive themselves, how they think others perceive them, how they react under stress, how they react to sudden noise, to kindness, to discipline.

No amount of willpower on our part is going to change the narrative of the brittle voice. Only when we accept that the brittle voice represents reality for our children can we start to gain their deep trust and attach with them at a more meaningful level. Then we can gently challenge the brittle voice and help our children to see themselves as good and lovable and worthy of a happy future. That's when the hard work really begins.

Empathy: that's what you need

Empathy can sound like a flaky concept, and coming from some mouths it is. It is a lot more than just kind words and a pat on the back though. It is about engaging on an emotional level with someone else and accepting that the way they experience the world may be different from ours but it is their truth. In my experience empathy is the key which unlocks our children. But real, deep, meaningful empathy takes courage and humility.

A child's paperwork, which contains details of their birth family and early history, can be a harrowing and distressing read for adopters. Once we have read all there is to read and listened to the child's social worker bring some of the details to life, we may want to put it all into a locked filing cabinet and never think about it again. That's certainly how I felt.

The problem with trying to 'lock up' the past is that no lock is strong enough to keep the past from spilling out all over the present and the future. If our children are ever to have the courage to face their pasts and develop a coherent understanding of who they are and where they've come from we must do it first and then hold their hands and journey into the past with them. If we show we are not up to it, then we risk proving to our child that their past (an intrinsic part of them) is too disgusting, too harrowing to look at.

No one would choose to think about what child abuse really means on a visceral level; what it sounds like, smells like, tastes like, feels like, looks like. As adopters we have to be able to confront the past with courage. We have to read and understand and imagine at a deep level in order that we can empathise with our child. 'He was neglected' can trip easily off the tongue. It is a sanitised version of reality. Neglect isn't just a dirty house and a bit of time spent alone. It isn't just occasional hunger. It isn't just a bit of shouting from an adjoining room. Neglect is emotional and physical torture and it impacts upon children profoundly.

So averse are we as a culture to really looking child neglect in the face that we have created fantasies and simplicities to make ourselves feel better about it. As adopters we hear many of them and they include: 'They won't remember what happened to them,' 'Children are so resilient, they'll get over it,' 'You shouldn't dwell on the past so much.' These easy fantasies are tempting to buy into but run roughshod over a child whose experience of the world is horrific. There are fantasies closer to home too, such as, 'They loved you very much and they did their best' and 'They just didn't know how to be good parents.' These statements may be true, but need to be explored in the wider context of children's extreme anger and sadness over what has happened to them. I tried these out on our son a few times who just looked at me with that expression that says, 'You haven't understood me at all.' 'I am going to get a gun, track them down and shoot them all dead,' he declared as I dithered on about how everyone tried their best. He worked hard to make me understand until finally I did, and now I am ashamed that I misunderstood him so catastrophically for so long.

I have had to look the neglect and the abuse, which haunts our family, full in the face, without looking away. It was and still is a horrible but necessary part of accessing the quality and amount of empathy that's needed for a life shared with a traumatised child. It is a large part of why parenting a traumatised child transforms us into better human beings.

Magic beads

The experience of living amongst and coming up against 'Trauma' is not an easy experience to describe but I'll try. Trauma feels like a thing, a being that stalks our house like an opportunistic and parasitic monster. Having shared my life with it for some years now I've got used to its wily, sneaky ways and I've got quite good at keeping one step ahead. It's still easy at times to confuse Trauma with the child, but they are different things. There is at all times a real, loving, beautiful child in there, even when they are all but obscured by Trauma. And if we're not careful, Trauma can come after us too and trick us into behaving in ways we would never have thought possible.

Trauma enjoys nothing more than shame and self-loathing. It feasts on them, so I've found it's best to try to reduce shame and self-loathing if you want to weaken Trauma. 'Is what I'm about to do or say likely to increase or decrease shame?' is a good test, and helps us to create the conditions in which Trauma fails to thrive. Trauma is a tricky opponent though, and will try to mask shame to look like wilful disobedience, or conscious insolence, or decisive rage. It's important not to let it fool you though, so try hard to keep the real child in mind.

Trauma was born out of abusive and neglectful parenting, and when we are tired and scared and hopeless it holds out a beautiful, shiny, magic bead in its grubby, gnarled hands and tempts us into creating the conditions it grew out of. How appealing that bead looks, how simple and easy. How satisfying might be the lecture we can attach to it, the lecture about being good and doing what they're told and acting more responsibly, which might make us feel better for a time but is actually all about blame.

I describe Trauma in this rather melodramatic fairytale style because that is how I've come to know it. It's a confidence trickster and has sent me running into the comfortable and familiar arms of traditional parenting methods many times, conned by the apparent simplicity, neatness and the purity of its mechanics. Each time I've been back there our family has come out worse, relationships are fractured, behaviours have spiralled out of control and children are left feeling bad, worthless and culpable. Home is no longer a sanctuary but has become a place of fear and loneliness. There's a clue in that last sentence as to where I'm going with this.

The problem with traditional parenting methods, and by that I mean the kind of training by removal, exclusion, sticker, bead, stern lecture or whatever, is that although Trauma may play along for a while, it will find the cracks in the system (every system has them) and exploit them. Within days or weeks of the trumpeted roll-out of the new system, you will find yourself marvelling at just how quickly your beautiful system collapsed under the weight of twisted logic and tenacity. Or alternatively Trauma may just stick two fingers up at the system and watch with delight as you ramp it up so high as to render it unworkable. It will sit on the naughty step and scream obscenities for hour upon hour and then laugh in your face; it will say, 'Take all my pocket money, take all my toys, take my bed, take my clothes, take my humanity'; it will never show remorse; it will never crack. It will crack you. If you try to play Trauma at it's own game, it will outgun you every time.

Of course nothing we can inflict upon our child will be any worse than what they have already experienced. They have learnt that adults are untrustworthy, that they take things from them, shout at them, deny them good times, leave them alone. We need to challenge that learning, not reinforce it by falling into the trap that Trauma has set for us. We need to be careful not to unthinkingly replicate the behaviour of the original perpetrators. That's my experience.

If magic beads and stickers and suchlike, or modified versions of them work in your family, then fine, but they don't work in mine or in lots of other adoptive families I've come across. If they were the simple antidote to Trauma they pretend to be, I don't think I'd have found myself staring into the deep chasm of adoption breakdown choking on my own vomit. I still get treated to the occasional lecture from the well-meaning about firmer boundaries and not putting up with things and reward systems and charts, as though Trauma has been a figment of my imagination, a product of my weak will and flaky temperament. You may do too.

As my own children get older and their emotional and psychological scars are healing, they are able to take some consequential thinking, but it's a slow process and must always have empathy and understanding at the heart. I've come to realise that where Trauma is concerned, if a solution looks too easy and sounds too easy (and comes with a bit of a power trip), then it usually is too easy. The downfall of course is when the too easy system fails and parents are left feeling hopeless and useless, and can find themselves being blamed for what really is a systemic failure. What has worked for us when nothing else has is real, painful, emotional engagement, deep understanding of trauma and its wily ways, the courage to see the world through our children's eyes and to be informed by what we see. If I had to simplify this, I'd say it's mainly about listening, not preaching. And empathy.

A book which I have found particularly useful on this subject is *Why Can't My Child Behave? Empathic Parenting Strategies That Work for Adoptive and Foster Families* by Dr Amber Elliot. It has helped me to understand that the behaviours we sometimes wish we could train out of our children are the very behaviours which helped them to survive impossibly difficult circumstances. Her approach is rather like teaching a drowning man to swim, rather than taking away his life jacket and giving him a telling off.

Elite parenting

For much of my adoption experience I was, I now realise, attempting to prop up a state of crumbling denial. At first life was hard because the children were settling in. Then it was hard because they were starting school, or moving up a class. Then perhaps it was hard because I was a substandard parent or I was lacking in perspective and all children are super-challenging to parent. Then it became blindingly, undeniably obvious that the reason I found myself on the kitchen floor sobbing into the onion skins and biscuit crumbs of life was because our children were profoundly traumatised by their pasts, and as a result I had no choice but to become an elite, therapeutic parent, and to think of myself as such.

Elite parenting is strenuous, relentless, stretching and lonely in a way that average parenting is not. The change in perspective from wishful to realistic thinking has for me been an important part of becoming competent. We start off, perhaps believing we've entered the flat 5km race, we didn't put on our best trainers, we didn't carb-load the day before, we didn't download the playlist entitled 'Motivational' on to our MP3 players and we didn't do much training. Part way through the road gets steep, there are no drinks stations and the streets are silent and empty of supporters. Then the cold realisation creeps through us: we've unwittingly entered a marathon and we're in the high Pyrenees and it's winter. The moment when I could no longer deny that I had inadvertently entered myself for a marathon was crushing. 'I can't do it. I don't want to do it. This is going to finish me. Why me? This is not my life' were my thoughts. I was a combination of distraught, angry and grief-stricken.

You may have prepared for the marathon and stood at the start line knowing exactly what to expect. I didn't. I suspect that most of us don't.

My advice is to get prepared. Go on every course you can get to, read every book you can get your hands on, watch every DVD and share experiences with other adopters. Be open to learning and never stop. Prepare for the worst and celebrate the wins. And don't forget to look after yourself (see Chapter 10, Self-Care).

Our children don't get to choose which race to run. We must run alongside them through the sunshine and the rain, down the slippery slopes and up the rocky climbs. I'm not yet sure how I'll get to the summit but I'm confident I will, and when I do I'll see you there and the views will be amazing.

CHAPTER 2

ESTABLISHING THE BASICS

Routine, routine, routine

A neglected child experiences a harsh unpredictability about the world they inhabit.

Food, warmth, cleanliness, quiet and calm, a loving touch, a loving gaze are randomly delivered and perhaps, for prolonged periods, not at all. A baby who experiences good care learns that it can relax into the comforting arms of predictability, never doubting that they are safe and loved. A cry of hunger equates to getting fed, a cry of tiredness equates to a warm, comfortable and quiet place to sleep. A baby who experiences poor early care learns that the world is inherently dangerous. A cry of hunger may or may not be ignored, a cry of tiredness may not result in the conditions which facilitate sleep. They become hard-wired not to trust others and take control of their own survival. I would love to report that a few months of dependable routine soothes and cures the self-sufficient infant, but in my experience, it does not.

Routine is the scaffolding which props our children up as they slowly learn that perhaps their new parents might just be capable of doing a half-decent job, sometime way out in the distant future. They take an awful lot of convincing. But, very slowly (painfully slowly it may seem) small pieces of the scaffolding can be removed without resulting in a collapse. Even then, they are going to demand that you are super-dependable. Fail to pick them up from school on time one day, or run out of milk one morning and you are the most terrible parent there ever was. That scaffolding better get reinforced while you prove yourself again.

Getting up

In our house the tone of the entire day can be determined by the first few moments of the morning – those first few moments when you are barely conscious and perhaps nursing a residual bitterness at being woken at 5.30am for the fifth consecutive morning, or still reeling from the dramas of the day before.

Irrespective of the baggage I wake up with, I have learnt the bountiful rewards of making myself greet both of our children with joy at the start of each day. Even now that they are older and I have to wake them up (drag them out of bed) on a school day, I do so gently and say something nice. They will often reach out a hand from under the duvet, seeking that first connection. Even if I am raging inside about being called a fat something or a freak loser the night before I still do it. 'Fake it 'til you make it' is my mantra. So too is 'Tomorrow is a new day'. Of course the day can still deteriorate at a frightening rate, but without the morning greeting in our house, all is lost. The same goes for a reconciliation after a day at school, or a day out without you – always greet them heartily and show them you are glad to see them back. 'I missed you' can go a long way. So too can 'I was thinking of you today.'

Getting dressed

According to some experts in the field, a four-year-old child is expected to be able to dress themselves unaided. If yours can't, then shame on you and furthermore, shame on you for sending them to school unable to carry out such a basic task where they just waste everybody's time.

Like many aspects of child rearing, those of us raising traumatised children must close our eyes and ears to what everyone else is doing and preaching.

'Oh my goodness, you've been up here for 45 minutes and you have only put one sock on. What have you been doing?' is something I admit has come out of my mouth.

The answer to that question is, 'I've been all alone and waiting for you to show me that you care for me,' if only they could tell us. Our children have missed so much nurture that we must sit with them as they dress or we must dress them ourselves, day after day, month after month, year after year, whatever it takes. Even our older children are still toddlers inside in many respects. I sometimes help my teenager to dress himself (he won't thank me for sharing that with you).

Mealtimes

To prevent society going to the dogs, families must all eat around a table together, once a day and at least half a mile from the nearest television. They should preferably engage in friendly conversation about how their day was and exchange opinions on the domestic and global news stories of the day, the relative merits of Keynesian versus free market economics and the state of modern British politics. Furthermore, children must learn the value of food by eating everything on their plate, including at least two portions of vegetables, one portion of oily fish and one portion of whole grains.

My inner parent, the one I've retrained but who still haunts my parenting from time to time, would wholeheartedly agree with the statement above. I've listened to enough 'Desert Island Discs' to know that the great and the good were shaped by stimulating family mealtime conversation. The therapeutic parent that I am being redesigned as can see it for what it is – a perfect storm. All the ingredients for conflict are there: food, control, close proximity, the weight of expectations inherited from family and society, memories, tiredness at the end of the day and particularly for children, feeling on display. It is no wonder that mealtimes can be a flashpoint.

'What are we having for tea?' is a question I used to get asked around 35 times a day. These days it's more like six times. It's all good and well saying, 'Take the pressure out of mealtimes' but the pressure is there all of its own accord in many adoptive families. The affects of prolonged hunger on a young child are, I think, vastly underestimated, and there is almost no advice around on how to cope with a child who is persistently anxious about food.

I have tried many different responses to the 'What are we having for tea?' question and none of them have worked in the long term. I've tried, 'I've pinned the menu on the fridge, go and take a look'; I've tried, 'Do you remember I told you we were having sausages?' 'Something nice' and 'Worms'. There are no magic solutions and so I try to respond truthfully and as calmly as possible. When I'm on good form I head the question off, 'Let me just tell you because I think you'll want to know that we are having sausages for tea today, sausages, yes sausages.' When I'm really not on good form, I might mutter 'sausages' and it will physically hurt to do so. On bad days I yell 'SAUSAGES!'

I have attempted over the years, as far as is humanly possible, to have tea on the table at roughly the same time every evening. I cook quite a narrow range of meals and if I go 'off-piste' with, say, a stir fry or something really exotic like a mild curry, then some pre-meal counselling and preparation is required, with reassurance that it doesn't have to be eaten. After many horrible meals ending in messy standoffs I now employ the 'You can choose not to eat it and get down from the table, or you can eat it and have some pudding.' I don't insist they eat something that they clearly find revolting so the rule is flexible. After much practice I am able to deliver this system with (almost) total calm and it has resulted in much more pleasant mealtimes than we used to have. I have been to other people's houses at mealtimes where children are allowed to wander around a bit and have toys at the table and it's all lovely and relaxed. This approach might work for you. It is a disaster in our house where a few mealtime rules are what holds back chaos. Without them it would be like Christmas dinner round at the Bullingdon Club.

As I've alluded to before, I had always pictured myself as the matriarch of a large, Bohemian family, where mealtimes were a dynamic and sociable eating and sharing fest. Nowadays the buffet meal is about the most stressful and undesirable experience one can have at the dinner table. Plates of food to share set off immediate stress responses which cause little hands to grab and mouths to be filled at speed. There is much counting and measuring and reporting of how many Kettle chips someone has had compared to someone else, or how many pieces of pizza and how big exactly they were and how many pieces of pineapple each one had on them. The shared meal is perhaps a required instrument of torture in order that our children learn worthy lessons like how to share, but personally I rarely have the mental capacity to survive such an experience in good spirits. What determines a good meal in our house is predictability and that means a meal, already served, with no leftovers. It's a long way from my Bohemian dream, but it works for us.

What also works for us, rather counter-intuitively, is going out for a meal. I wondered if this was just a Donovan phenomenon, but it seems it may not be, as I know other adopters who report the same. Our children are a dream whenever we go out and eat in a pub or a restaurant. So good are they, that we have been complimented by diners sat at neighbouring tables. It isn't even as though the stress of eating out is being held in and saved for later. Our children genuinely enjoy eating out and are calm when we get home afterwards. It is nice to bask in a little bit of parental glory every once in a while, and I most shamefully admit that I have to try very hard not to glare at other people's children as they race noisily around eating establishments being annoying.

During difficult times, mealtimes in our house may, contrary to advice on routines, become much more *laissez-faire* occasions. If an angry child finds it easier to eat by themselves at the kitchen table either before or after everyone else, then that's what happens. If they refuse to eat then I give them the choice not to eat anything. Depending on how they are, I might later offer them something small. 'Here, I thought you might be hungry and I know you've had a difficult day' can show you've connected with how they are feeling. They may have rejected the meal in a rage, regretted it later and be in a state of hunger and shame. Hunger and shame is not a place we want them to be and certainly not because we have dug in our heels over a routine.

Sometimes anxiety at mealtimes can show itself as silly or bizarre behaviour. A personal favourite of mine is the acting out, at the dinner table, of a bizarre scenario, with ridiculous voices. I'm sure you will have your favourite too. Though this may not be a very therapeutic response, when I'm hearing about Barry the snake and his tutu made of caramel and buttons that talk, I have to make my apologies and leave the table. I know, not very playful of me, but in our house there is a subtle difference between bizarre and playful. They are heading to entirely different destinations.

Anxiety over food can show itself as a need to consume food quickly and in great quantities. Without going into too much detail this can present not only challenges to little digestive systems, but to the household plumbing too. Again I don't believe there is a magic solution to rushed eating, other than years and years of dependable mealtimes and reassurance that we will never let our children go hungry. Sometimes I make sure to provide a meal that needs a bit of chewing just to slow things down a bit. I also act as a remote 'full' button. I mostly regulate on behalf of one of our children although very occasionally I let her eat as much as she wants so she can experience what feeling very, very full is like. I might interject now and again and say something like, 'Let's pause for a moment and see what our tummies feel like'. It doesn't always work, but there is a definite improvement.

If I could offer one piece of advice about mealtimes and food it would be this – as far as you can, keep the emotion out. I have learned this the hard way. Calmness around food is the only way to go, even if it means sacrificing some long-held beliefs about five-a-day or clean plates or interesting political discourse.

Bedtime

Bedtime can be the biggest hurdle of the day, coming as it does, most inconveniently, at the end of the day when everyone is tired and fractious. It is tempting to cut corners, but scrimp on the bedtime routine and you pay for it in spades.

I confess that I have been a stickler for bedtimes. If I'm going to last the course as an elite parent then I need a rest in the evening and a decent sleep. When I'm tired *everyone* suffers. Either I get enough sleep, or I can't therapeutically parent. This is not a mix and match situation.

Obviously our children need a predictable, reliable and relaxing bedtime routine but I'm not going to preach to you about things you already know. Anyway, if it was as easy as that, therapeutic parenting would be a breeze, and it isn't.

For many of our children bedtime is a scary transition from the activity and company of the day, to the inactivity, darkness and separation of the night. Night time may have negative associations for children who have been neglected. Perhaps it was the time when cries were ignored, nappies were left unchanged, hunger pangs were felt or abuse was inflicted. The house may have been full of unknown adults and loud and frightening noises. It is no wonder that many of our children struggle at bedtime and during the night.

Children who operate on high alert all day, as many of our children do, get very tired. They may well need to go to bed earlier than their peers and wake up later. For some children, however, it isn't that easy to switch off and recharge, they seem to remain in a state of high alert all night and will be woken by the hoot of an owl or a stealthy parent standing on a creaky stair. These are the sorts of children you need around you if you are sleeping under the stars in bear country.

One of our children woke every night perhaps five, six or seven times for a very long time. Before we knew it we were all on our knees with exhaustion and our therapeutic capacities were nil. We felt we had tried everything. We went into her room every ten minutes to calm her and we crept out and that made no different at all. We went in without looking at her or talking to her and that made things worse. I sat in the room with her, and that didn't help either. Perhaps I should have slept in her room with her, but I know that I could not have done that and maintained halfway decent service as a parent. The only factor that really made any difference was time. She learnt through our repetitive actions that her cot was no longer a place of abandonment.

Something that ruins bedtimes for me is the tyranny of the school reading book. You must apparently read with your children every evening, which is fine if they want to read but can be just about the last straw if they don't. For children who find school difficult, being reminded of it at bedtime isn't that conducive to sleep. What they need at bedtime is attachment, I think. If they can experience that by reading with you, then great, but if they need to lie in bed with you and watch *The Great British Bake Off* then that's great too. Teachers might make alternative suggestions such as reading with your child as soon as they get home from school. I don't need to explain to you why this is not a workable solution for many of our children. I have developed a few sneaky strategies around the school reading book and reading record. My favourite is to read a big chunk together on a calm evening and then fill out the reading record as though we'd read a few pages every evening. Sometimes I've even pretended we've read when we haven't, or we pick a book we've read before. Cheating? Perhaps, but if the result is calmer bedtimes, then in my book that's allowed.

Bedtime in our house can also be disclosure time. There is something about that murky join between day and night which provides the right conditions for sharing difficult things. When this happens I ask my husband to record *Downton Abbey* then sit and listen and forget the time. Of course a child may be trying to put off bedtime by coming up with something in the hope we will get suckered in. You get to learn the difference between the two. When you think you are being suckered in I find something like, 'I know you'd like to talk for a while longer and so would I but it is time for sleeping now and I will be ready to listen in the morning' works better than, 'Go to sleep, *Downton Abbey* is about to start.'

As the years have passed I have learned to relax a bit over bedtimes. There are often rumblings after lights out and the need to pass that wee which has been especially stored up for the purpose. I mostly ignore it now and it mostly settles down. If the situation starts to get worse over a few nights then I sit on the landing with a book and a small gin and occasionally bark, 'Back to bed' (therapeutically of course).

Older children may put an extraordinary amount of effort into secreting their mobile phone or other device into their bed so that they may then stay awake into the small hours using said device and then torture us with their tiredness the following day. I can hear the cries of, 'They all do that' and yes, you may be right. All I will say is the determination, forward planning, creativity and acting skills employed by our children are top class. Be vigilant. Be very vigilant. And look out for that glow coming from underneath the bedroom door – it's a dead giveaway.

Expecting the unexpected

Saying that surprises don't go down well in our house would be putting it mildly. A surprise can mean buying a different toothpaste or the phone ringing at an unusual time of the evening or me having had a haircut. All of these events frighten the horses and can add an unusual energy into the day. For years I have provided watered down apple juice as a drink with the occasional cup of Ribena on special occasions. Several months ago, in an unexplainable off-the-wall moment, I bought some Fruit Shoots. It was as though the natural order of the universe had been turned on its head and the comforting blankets of space and time were about to unravel. The Fruit Shoots became an obsession. When are we going to drink the Fruit Shoots? Can I have a Fruit Shoot? Can I have another Fruit Shoot? Can I have one in my lunchbox? What will happen when the Fruit Shoots run out? There was an evening raid on the Fruit Shoots and several bottles that appeared to be unopened were, in fact, empty. I know that our children need to become accustomed to change, but after two days of Fruit Shoot mania I resolved never to buy them again. This episode demonstrated to me that even after years of predictability, the unexpected can still present a challenge.

Boring, boring, boring is how life has to be on most fronts in order for normal service to be maintained. Sometimes I find the boringness really gets to me and I feel a physical need to get drunk, wear yellow, dye my hair green, go to a festival with no showers, dance the crazy dance, eat something with too many chillies in and indulge in risky substances. Crazy these days means a visit to the ice cream factory in Pizza Hut, or not wearing a coat when it looks like it might rain or buying Fruit Shoots instead of apple juice.

As our children grow up and feel more secure, they will become more resilient in coping with the unexpected. Their resilience is nourished by the growing medium of boringness and predictability, even if ours is not.

We can't always protect our children from the unexpected and over time they will need to learn and practise coping strategies. I know families who successfully manage the unexpected by springing it upon their children with no warning. In our house this method fails big time. We have to prepare the ground for a surprise very carefully and repeatedly, but the hard work is now reaping benefits. Our children will tell us when they are worried about going to a party for example, or to somebody's house, and will ask us to talk them through exactly what is going to happen. They help us to understand what they need in order to cope with the situation. I'm not sure we would have been able to make this progress and achieve this level of trust if we had always sprung surprises on them.

Slave to the rhythm

The scaffolding of routine shouldn't only be built around daily activities, but around less frequently occurring activities too. I've found it important to establish firm weekly, monthly, termly and annual routines which tap out the rhythms of time. Young children seem to enjoy fixing time against small events such as bin lorry day or shopping day. It may help to underline these small but insignificant events to give them extra meaning. If a child, like mine, puts particular importance on bin day then you could sort the recycling together, take the box out to the pavement and look out for the lorry. Shopping day could mean buying doughnuts to share for tea. In our family Friday means Friday sweets which we have after school and which mark the beginning of the weekend. It is important to ring fence these small rituals and not to allow them to be raided for purposes of punishment. Regular shared rituals build up feelings of safety and security, and using them as bargaining chips can devalue them and make our children feel as though the good times have to be earned. They don't. Our children deserve the good times.

These small rituals allow the week to develop a comforting pattern, a means of placing oneself in time and navigating a way through its landmarks. Having a rhythm to the day and the week also means that some improvisation can start to take place around it, which takes me neatly on to the next section. How's that for rhythm?

CHAPTER 3

THIS IS MEANT TO BE FUN

Weekends

'Hooray, it's the weekend' is sometimes an unrealistic sentiment when you share your life with a traumatised child. Let's face it, although this may not be a very parentally correct statement to make, weekends can be hell. Weekends can make you look forward to *Countryfile* and *Antiques Roadshow*, not because they're any good, but because they mean Sunday evening. Weekends can make you beg for Monday morning to come around.

The trouble with weekends (or what I used to enjoy about them) is they aren't all that predictable. Radio alarm clocks are switched to 'OFF', school timetables are put aside, the words 'lie in' are flirted with and there we are contemplating two days of empty, frightening leisure time. Without the rhythm of a Monday to Friday, Saturdays and Sundays can feel like a structureless jelly or a long piece of meaningless improvisation. To us that may sound brilliant, to our children it can be unsettling. So how can we wedge some relaxation into the weekend, but still keep enough structure to ensure everyone stays on the tracks?

I am terrible at this so I'm going to talk about what I aim to do but often forget to. If my children are like yours then they will be concerned about what the weekend holds in store. 'What are we doing this weekend?' is a question I get asked many, many times over starting on around a Wednesday morning. Wherever there is repeated questioning, therein lies a possible anxiety. 'What are we doing this weekend?' probably translates as, 'I have nothing to hang on to and I feel a bit scared; for goodness sake tell me what I can expect.'

If we're not careful then our need for two days of structureless fun and relaxation can conflict with our child's need for everything to be planned out (and vice versa).

Weekends for us can be like a complicated improvisation. It's important to have a few things that we do quite frequently – a woodland walk, a visit to a cafe in a nearby town, a visit to the park, a trip to the cinema, some baking. These are things that our children feel secure doing, enjoy doing and can relax into, like a basic chord progression. Of course they rely on some unknowns, like the weather and how everyone is operating and whether there are any free tables in the cafe and if there are any other plans for the weekend (the fiddly improvised bits).

The adults in our house will usually form a rough plan for the weekend on a Friday and share it so that no one wakes up to a void of frightening emptiness on Saturday morning. The rough plan though is usually flexible. Sometimes a child will wake up looking utterly exhausted and will plead to be able to stay at home. Sometimes a child will (how can I put this politely?) 'fall out of bed on the wrong side', and encouraging them into clothes and out of the house is a battle of wills. We've learned to read the mood music and improvise accordingly. Occasionally one can play 'Call My Bluff':

'When are we going out then?' might come the frost-coated question, which follows a good hour of refusals and worse.

'We've decided not to.'

'WHAT? But I really, really, really want to and YOU SAID we were going out.'

'OK then, put your shoes on and if you call me a ****** ****** again then we're staying in.'

I don't believe that empathy and head stroking is appropriate in all circumstances, but more of that later.

Of course it doesn't always work, but this is the sort of improvisation that we use in our house frequently. It is part of the reason why I could sometimes fall asleep standing up.

Offering a limited choice of activities is universally considered to be a 'good thing'. It cons children into believing they have some control. It is something that can work marvellously with one child, but try it with two or more and you can wave goodbye to the weekend. As our family consists of one child per adult we sometimes plan to do things separately and give each child a choice. It is remarkable how often they choose the same thing and then we can pursue the original objective which was to all go out as a family. (Another little dance routine that we perform to keep the show on the road.)

When a child expresses a desire to do something in particular, something that they are really keen to do, like see a film or visit a donkey sanctuary, then we do our best to accommodate that desire. A sibling may take against the idea, not because they don't want to do the activity, but because their sibling really does. These situations have to be played by ear I think. There are times when encouragement can be used and times when it can't.

Sometimes, just sometimes, I might really want to go somewhere or do something in particular at the weekend. I will convince myself that I shouldn't always have to do child-centred stuff, that they should learn that sometimes we all have to compromise and perhaps they might enjoy a ten-mile walk or a shopping trip. Now, let me count how many towns I've dragged a sulky child around, how many country walks have been blighted. I've concluded that if the emotional weather forecast is set to sulky or stormy then there really is no point. On return to the car after the last hideous walk I dragged everyone on, someone had the cheek to say, 'I actually enjoyed that.' I am getting better at ignoring the public dramas (and other people's reactions to the public dramas). And I get to say irritatingly stupid things like, 'Isn't this more fun than playing on the Xbox all day?'

There are those who advise that the usual bedtime routine should be stuck to every day including Saturdays and Sundays. It is great advice. I don't follow it. I might do if the day has been horrible, as much to hurry on a peaceful evening as to offer structure and routine, but generally I don't have the will to run my entire life like clockwork. No, weekend bedtimes in our house are a bit later, a bit freer and don't feature anything out of the school book bag. We might all watch some silly television together or put on a DVD. It is the weekend after all.

School holidays

There are two ways to play school holidays. One is to produce a rough timetable, populate it as far as you can with plans and stick it on the fridge. The other is to hold control and let the children know what is happening on a daily basis. I know adopters who use the second method to great effect as knowledge of future plans stress out their children too much. I use the first method, the rough timetable. If I didn't I would hear the question, 'What are we doing tomorrow?' or many other versions of it so frequently I would by now be living in a hut on a remote island off the coast of Finland. On my own.

I might kick off 'Operation Holiday Timetable' a week or so before the holidays start, with a casual conversation about what everyone would like to do in the holidays. It might start with something like:

> 'I'm really looking forward to spending some time with you over the holidays, what shall we do together?'

There will generally be lots of outlandish and expensive suggestions but there will also be some good ones too. I add in a few of my own. I compile a list, nothing formal and neat (I'm not talking spreadsheet here) and sometimes the children will add their own ideas with illustrations. I find it useful to include a few 'out there' suggestions ('alright, you'd like to go whale-watching off the Falkland Islands, let's get that one down') so that the list doesn't become a stick to beat ourselves with, or a stick for others to beat us with.

Then I hand draw a table with days of the week across the top and morning and afternoon down the side. I write in the fixed activities (arrangements to meet people, holidays, clubs and suchlike) and add in a few low-key activities and perhaps a couple of trips out. So I might put in 'Go to the library,' 'Visit Granny and Grandad' and 'Donkey Sanctuary?' The question mark is very important. The question mark says, 'Things might change.' There may be entire days which have nothing in them except a question mark. The question mark is for some an uncomfortable fact of life and for those of us who don't cope well with over-organisation, a blessed relief. It is worth having the question mark conversation before the holidays start. Something like this might work:

'I can understand that you like to know everything that will happen because it's a bit scary seeing a day with a question mark in.'

They may look at you like you are crazy or you may get a slight hint of agreement, in which case you might be able to take the conversation on:

'Sometimes we don't know what we will do on the question mark days until they get a bit closer. But if the question marks are making you feel a bit wobbly then you tell me.'

Once you have successfully navigated everyone across the unknown you might be able to reflect back:

'You coped really well with that question mark day. I enjoyed going to the park with you, it was a nice surprise.'

It's these short reflective conversations that help to build resiliency around the unknown.

Before the holidays start I get prepared. I buy art materials, ingredients for baking, some books and some DVDs. I don't spend a fortune but I have learnt that time spent getting prepared is never time wasted. I keep my holiday stash hidden and produce items when I need to.

The holidays always include days when trouble is clearly building just beneath the surface like a super-volcano. Scratchy days. Days when nothing is right, or good enough, days when it is fun to wind everyone up and watch them fire, days when you've already taken everyone swimming and to the doughnut shop and there are still hours and hours to fill, days when you feel like running away. For these days you need to take everyone by surprise and sort of shock them into a different groove, and one way of doing this is by producing something from your holiday stash. At the same time as you produce the DVD or whatever it is, try saying:

'I saw this in the supermarket last week and I thought of you.'

I can hear the doubters. It's rewarding bad behaviour, right? They need to be taught that bad behaviour is unacceptable? All I will say is, that itchy feeling that our children get, the itch that can't be scratched, the itch that sends them and us a bit loopy, well that itch needs to be calmed. They can't help the itch and if we don't help them to a soothing activity then the itch can grow into something much worse.

If the 'something much worse' does happen and the day is a total disaster then write it off. If there is something to be learnt from it then learn it and move on but do not blame yourself. Learning to parent a traumatised child is like learning a new language. If we try something and it fails then remember the mantra 'Tomorrow is a new day.'

A random topic here but for me a holiday life-saver: the scooter. The scooter is the best investment we ever made in family harmony. The scooter can be taken to any flattish surface, it folds up and can be carried and it fits easily into the boot of a car. It is fun, doesn't take much skill to ride and doesn't require any additional equipment. The scooter has saved our sanity on many occasions. So if a day looks like it's panning out badly and it's not raining too hard, we reach for the scooters.

Holidays can be arduous for traumatised children, but they are also arduous for us, their parents. I hear they can be hard on all parents (boo hoo) but it is different for the parents of traumatised children. There are many reasons for this. Our children, scared by long, unstructured rivers of time, can show us their most challenging behaviours during the holidays. We may witness behaviours we've never encountered before, and being on the back foot during the holidays when there is no time to recuperate and less support around than usual can be exceptionally demanding. Our children often find themselves socially isolated and the holidays remind them of this isolation. They may be the only child who is not invited to play at someone's house or at the park and it is hurtful. Small children may not be aware of all they are missing out on but older children will become very keenly aware and can react by getting angry or withdrawn. Empathy is the best way, that and encouraging friendships where it's appropriate to do so. Other than that we can find ourselves being parent *and* best friend to them. It's a big ask, especially as they reach the age when they feel they want to be gaining some independence. Their behaviour may be pushing us away one moment and then wanting us to play football with them the next.

The long summer holidays in particular can feel like running a marathon a day for six weeks. Sadly I have no magic wand I can offer, but do flick ahead to Chapter 10, Self-Care, if you are finding the holidays particularly hard-going.

One thing I used to dread about the end of the holidays was the post-holiday school playground analysis. It is absolutely only acceptable when asked how your holidays were to reply with

100 per cent positivity. Saying, 'Actually the holidays were shit' in a primary school playground is like standing at the bar of your local pub and telling everyone, 'I've just visited the STD clinic.' In these situations I lie, thank my lucky stars that I survived the holidays and go home and eat a block of chocolate and wallow in the glorious sound of silence ringing in my ears. It's perfectly acceptable to look forward to the beginning of term.

One of our children found the school holidays traumatic for many years. As he's got older he's concluded that the holidays are actually pretty good compared to the alternative: school. He now functions better during the holidays than during term-time. On the last day of term he looks as though a weight has been lifted from his shoulders. This is some measure of progress (I think) and reminds me that situations are never fixed.

High days and holidays

Christmas, Easter, Mother's Day, birthdays, Halloween, adoption anniversaries: how those words fill me with panic. Each one comes with its own set of complicated and unique challenges. I'll start with, what's for me, the most panic-inducing.

Christmas

I must now let you into a secret which risks causing you to think the worst of me. I apologise in advance if you are one of those strange beings who enjoy spending half the year obsessing about Christmas. I am a Christmas humbug.

I am not religious, but this is not why I take against the season. I dislike enforced shopping and profligate spending. I dislike waste, I dislike crowds, I dislike being told when and how I should make merry, I dislike Christmas television and I dislike sitting around indoors feeling hot and above all else, I dislike, nay detest, being reminded of Christmas in September when I am desperately trying to cling on to summer. I know it's unforgiveable. I don't know anyone else like me. Correction, I *didn't* know anyone else like me until our eldest child arrived. As far as sulking through the silly season goes, we are a match made in heaven.

It took me many years to realise that he was a Christmas humbug too, because he was too little to tell me and he too had picked up on the vibe that to dislike Christmas is the social equivalent of having rabies. One Christmas I shared my guilty secret with him and his eyes lit up.

'That's exactly how I feel,' he said.

'You do? You're not just saying that to please me?'

'No. I like to get a few presents but not too many and I like to see some people on Christmas Day and I like mince pies and that's it.'

My dear boy, that was music to my ears.

He went on to describe how he hates the fuss and the build up, the pressure to be sociable when you don't feel like it, the lack of freedom to sit on your own if you want to.

'It's too busy and noisy,' he said.

Christmas these days is pretty much tailored to him (and me!). It was never a particularly high-octane occasion in our house, but it is definitely low key. Gone are the times of high drama and spectacular meltdown. I had inadvertently reached out to him and given him permission to explain why Christmas is difficult for him and shown empathy for his experience. I can't claim the glory for this because it was entirely accidental.

It was a lesson to me. It was a lesson in pushing aside everyone else's expectations and listening to the child. I may have learnt it by accident, but it taught me to listen and watch much more carefully and to ask a few gentle questions. It was also a lesson in acceptance.

In any social situation, particularly during Christmas and other important festivals, it is useful to let our child know beforehand that they have an escape route. Trying a conversation like, 'If you find this party difficult then just find me and we'll find somewhere quiet together' and 'I may check on you if you seem like you are struggling' may be all that's needed to soothe a worry. This has worked well for us, not just because it establishes an escape route, but also because it has opened up communication around all sorts of difficult feelings. This helps children to build coping mechanisms which is really what all of us bar the most outgoing do to get through a particularly noisy party or a stressful visit to someone's house. The stress can come from the expectation for children to behave in a certain way, or from being around particularly energetic children, or from lots of noise. I guess it's about not judging what is or isn't stressful by our own stress reactions but by our child's.

There is a greater risk, I think, that our children become lost to us at Christmas and during other celebrations. We get absorbed in preparing food, chatting to friends and family and we may take a glass or two of sherry and become louder and laugh more than usual and then round off the day with a nap on the sofa. Our child can get forgotten a bit on a day that may be extra stressful for them.

Even those of us with straightforward histories are likely to reflect on the past at significant times of the year like Christmas. We may think about family members who have passed away or whom we don't see any more and we think about what Christmas was like for us as a child. I don't think it is any different for our children, especially if they recall spending Christmas with birth family members. It might be a bittersweet time for them as it is for many of us. That's not to say that we can't create our own traditions, traditions which don't stick doggedly to what we did as children, but which are made to measure our own families and which help to bind us together.

One tradition that we have had to ditch is Father Christmas. 'Father Christmas is a large bearded man who creeps into your bedroom at night when you're asleep' is not a line you might want to take with adopted children. To adults he might be a bit of fun and light fantasy, but to a traumatised child he might embody all their worst nightmares. I'm not suggesting that we take the fun out of Christmas, just that we have to be mindful.

Our eldest child rumbled Father Christmas at around age four and was mightily relieved when we confirmed that he was right, that the big, bearded one was in fact imaginary. There is then of course the problem of them keeping the illusory nature of Father Christmas from all the other children who still believe. Traumatised children are not good at keeping these kinds of secrets and I think it is unfair of us to expect them to do so. I've got no tips for dealing with that particular dilemma other than developing bad hearing and a loud cough to cover up any Father Christmas-related disclosures. Parents of 'normal' children can get snakey about the whole 'Your son upset my son by telling him that Santa doesn't exist' thing, for which I can only recommend a shallow apology and further development of the rhino hide of adoption.

And of course the other problem with Father Christmas is he feeds into our modern day obsession with rewards and sanctions. In the lead-up to Christmas, how many times do you hear parents say to children, 'If you don't start behaving Father Christmas won't bring you any presents' or 'Father Christmas only brings presents to good children'? I'm going to stick my neck out here and declare that I dislike that approach with all children and particularly adopted children. They deserve to have a few presents at Christmas, full stop. Christmas should not have to be earned, neither is it some kind of parental power trip.

Try as we might to limit Christmas to the 25th and 26th of December, it is as impossible a task as holding back the tide. It starts on the first of December and what would the Christmas period be without a meltdown or two over an advent calendar? Advent calendars are uniquely designed to torture traumatised children (and their parents) being as they are all about delayed gratification. I don't know when we decided that delayed gratification was a suitable stick to beat children with (possibly around the time of the Puritans), but our children in particular can fail at it spectacularly. And instead of just being cheesy pictures hidden behind windows, the advent calendar now comes with chocolate or toys which make delaying gratification even harder. Brilliant. If I was Queen of All Things, advent calendars would have windows with pictures behind them and nothing else. This would avoid a lot of the sneaking around and guerrilla tactics and the resulting meltdowns.

Here's what I do, although it doesn't always work. I buy two advent calendars for each child; one which contains chocolate and one which is trinket-free. I keep the chocolate calendars hidden and bring them out after our evening meal. Our older child keeps his trinket-free calendar in his bedroom because he likes to (but this doesn't remove all possibilities that windows will be criminally opened). Our younger child keeps her trinket-free calendar in the kitchen but will open a lot of her windows on the wrong days. That used to bother me. It doesn't anymore. I now give her the option of doing that. On 1 December I say something like, 'I know it's really hard to wait to open each window and sometimes the temptation to open them all is too strong, so if you want to open all the windows, that's all right.' This is the kind of thinking that typifies therapeutic parenting. If you find yourself falling into, 'Well all other children seem to be able to manage it' type thinking, then stop yourself. They are not 'all other children'.

Going on holiday

Holidays, the going away type, have to be carefully stage-managed in our family. Travelling, arriving somewhere unfamiliar, sleeping in a different bed are all enough on their own to blow the mind of a traumatised child. It is an important time to really try to see the world through their eyes. Although they will probably never come out and say it, they will be worrying that they are about to be cast out from the family and abandoned in the airport, on the beach or in the middle of Disneyworld. They probably won't only be worrying a little bit, they will be terrified. 'Seven sleeps and then we'll be going back home' is meaningless to most small children. I wish I'd appreciated this early on.

I have learnt though experience that our best holidays involve as little excitement as possible. Hiring a holiday cottage near the beach and playing on the beach every day and having an ice cream from the same vendor at the same time every day worked well. Flying to Switzerland, staying in the mountains and putting our children into a holiday club for half the week did not. That's not to say that our more adventurous holidays weren't without enjoyment, but they caused a fair amount of distress and were not restful. What we manage these days is a static caravan in France, which we reach by ferry and car. The caravan has to be on a small, quietish campsite, which is impossible to escape from. It has to have three bedrooms because two children sharing a room is so stressful as to render the holiday experience void. We mainly walk to the local beach and go to the campsite pool. Perhaps twice during the holiday we will go to a supermarket which will make us all feel like murdering each other. We eat very simply and might have a couple of barbeques, which is about as wild as it gets.

Going away has to be the focus of much mental preparation beforehand. It is useful to share brochures, photographs and maps and to remember past holidays together with particular emphasis on the coming home. 'We go away for a short time and we always return home afterwards' is worth repeating (and repeating and repeating) I think.

As with so many aspects of therapeutic parenting it is worth reflecting after a trip away on what has worked and what hasn't worked. If you come home feeling cross because your child has ruined the holiday with their behaviour, then just maybe they weren't ready for it, or it needs to be scaled back. They don't mean to ruin things so try really hard not to take it personally.

There are times when we as adoptive parents and wage-earners and cooks and cleaners desperately need a break. If your children can manage a few days in a holiday club then why not try it, or if there are holidays clubs on offer closer to home, perhaps at school, then why not treat yourself to a mini-break at home? Therapeutic parenting is an intense experience and sometimes we need to recover our energies for the long run. I cover this in more detail in Chapter 10, Self-Care.

Easter

I sense that adopted children engage in Easter with more genuine fun and enjoyment than Christmas, and you may notice it with other religious festivals too. Perhaps it's the fluffy bunnies, the daffodils, the chicks and the chocolate, or perhaps it's that Easter is just allowed to be. There is less of a weight of expectation bearing down on Easter and less of a build up. The weather is usually picking up by then and for those of us whose children need a run around and a blast of fresh air everyday, this comes as a welcome relief.

The baking and making at Easter is also less stressful, I find. Anyone can melt a bar of chocolate, stir in some cornflakes, spoon the mix into a cake case and shove a chick and a mini-egg on top. Other than that, there's shop-bought hot cross buns to toast and copious amounts of chocolate to scoff. As far as return on effort, for me, Easter wins over all the high days.

Easter also seems freer of expectations too, and we can develop our own Easter traditions to suit our families. Every year I buy lots of cheap chocolate mini-eggs, chicks and rabbits and hide them in very hard to find places around the garden. We usually have additional children over at Easter and so they all head off in search of the hard to find chocolate and are gone for ages. The hiding places are sneaky and not necessarily easier for bigger, faster children to discover. It is interesting to watch the change in power balance playing out (and I also happen across chocolate while I'm weeding or hedge trimming months later, which is always a delightful bonus).

Perhaps the only sore point at Easter (depending on cultural background and triggers) is food and in particular chocolate, if you have a child with anxiety around food. Some children will not be able to rest until all the chocolate in the house has been consumed. It is not only children with a history of neglect who exhibit this behaviour. I confess that I, too, am driven to eat chocolate, or at least to think about it obsessively, if I know it is in the house. This gives me the therapeutic edge over those of you who eat bird-like amounts of your Easter egg at a time and still have some left over for the summer holidays.

Most of the time we may find ourselves having to control how much food our anxious children consume to prevent them eating until they are ill. They appear to lack a 'full indicator' and can literally eat until they are sick. I don't say this with any evidence behind me at all, but sometimes I think it's useful to ease off on controlling their food intake. So at Easter I don't hover over the 'stop' button quite so diligently and allow them to take the reins. I may occasionally say, 'Let's pause for a moment and check how we feel' and then let them take the reins again. We usually end up missing a meal or two as a result, or having some fruit instead of a meal, but I figure that it's only a day or two a year. It's also healthy for us to shut up our inner food dictators every once in a while.

Mother's Day and Father's Day

I wonder how many of us looked forward with misty eyes to the day when a small child would present us with a beautiful handmade card and a small gift on Mother's Day or Father's Day. If these days have lived up to your expectations then I am very happy for you and please do not read on or tell me about it.

If Mother's and/or Father's Day is now one of the most hideous times in your family's calendar then I feel your pain. In our house they are shit and I wish they would just go and drown themselves in a big bunch of yellow carnations.

The catch with Mother's or Father's Day is that it pushes in everyone's faces all that yet-to-work-through life history, all the loss and pain and grief, and then tries to cover it up with a box of Maltesers. It really is a crap of a day.

Children reminded of the pain they are burdened with may react in a variety of ways. They may refuse to engage in whatever has been planned, or they may be angry and rude. If they have siblings they may become hyper-competitive in proving who loves Mum or Dad the best. If we, their parents, also hold an idealised expectation of what these days should be, then we have all the ingredients for a raging forest fire.

Here's where the problem starts. We expect and hope for a lie in. We look forward to our lie in, fantasise about it and may even stay up late the night before in preparation for it. Our children may wake up early fizzing with the expectation of giving us their carefully crafted card and present and may not be able to stop themselves from waking us up. They will not understand and appreciate the sanctity of a lie in and will misread our irritation at being woken up earlier than usual as, 'Mum doesn't like me, I am worthless.'

In sibling households the competitiveness will have started days before. There will have been arguments about who hands Mum or Dad their present first, who has put more kisses and love hearts in their card and basically who loves (and is loved by) Mum or Dad the most. There are no winners.

If Mother's or Father's Day doesn't go swimmingly in your family then this is what you could try. The day, or a few days before, you could announce the following: 'Look, tomorrow is Mother's/Father's Day. I know it's a complicated day for you and sometimes it's a difficult day and it brings up some painful feelings so here's what we'll do…'

This year I'm planning to go to bed early the night before Mother's Day so I can be up early. Mr D. (or I) will have bought two almost identical cards and two almost identical presents and I will graciously accept those cards and presents, no matter how they are offered. We will then go out and have a late and greasy breakfast together because we all enjoy doing that and because staying in all day is a challenge when everyone is hurting. That's the plan anyway.

Many of our children are not yet ready to acknowledge that these days brings up difficult feelings, but I have found it useful to voice it, even if they don't want to go there. It's like saying, 'Your feelings are perfectly acceptable' and what better gift from a parent to a child.

Birthdays

If there is a theme developing around high days and holidays, then it is about keeping things low key. Developmentally traumatised children, as we know, find it difficult to regulate their emotions. A birthday can blow all the fuses of regulation and create an enormous and very public mess.

It is important to be guided by what a child is able to cope with on their birthday. Have a really good think about whether they really want the whole of their class running around them in the local soft play centre, whether or not two bin bags of presents is going to blow their minds, whether 'Happy Birthday' sung at them in public is something they will take in their stride. You might conclude that they can take all this in their stride. My point is, don't feel you have to do it just because everyone else does. Again and again therapeutic parenting is about really putting our children first, and that sometimes comes at the expense of other people's vicarious wishes.

In some families there is an expectation that a birthday will mean visitations en masse, piles of presents and bucket loads of fuss. You may find yourself in the unenviable position of having to put your child's needs ahead of others, and it's not always an easy thing to do. A conversation with a parent-in-law about why they shouldn't just pop in with their neighbour and best friend and a five foot tall teddy to surprise (shock) your traumatised child with is one of life's most tricky ones. You will no doubt be perceived as making this stand for selfish and melodramatic reasons. Being a strong and not always popular advocate is part of the job description. It is like exercise though, difficult at first, but with practice it gets easier. Over time those around you will come to realise that you were right all along, it just might take them a while to get there. If they don't come to realise that, you will develop a thick enough skin that you will no longer give a shit.

Something which can catch us on the back foot is how difficult our own birthdays can be for our children. In the same way that Mother's Day backfires, our own birthdays come with some expectations of being spoilt a bit and not having to be the cook and bottle-washer. I'm not sure whether it is overwhelming jealousy, a change in routine or a worry that we will be lost to them for the day as we wallow in birthdayness, but there can be a tendency for the Birthday Ruination Guerrilla Army to come out and do its worst. I know from experience that when times are tough and you've looked forward to some birthday wonderfulness only for it to be sabotaged, it can make you feel murderous. 'They can't even let me enjoy my birthday' is a thought that may sweep across your mind, along with images of donkeys buckling under a load to which a final straw has been added. It can make you want to cry in a wallow of self-pity.

Here's what we do in our family to balance the needs of children with an already frazzled adult who would really like to enjoy their birthday. The adults book the birthday day off work. If the birthday day falls upon a weekend then the nearest, most convenient week day is booked off work. The adults drop the children at school, pre-school, Aunty Geraldine's, Uncle Bernard's (delete as appropriate) and then head off somewhere lovely for the day or as much of the day as can be managed. The adults will sit in cafes, laugh, hold actual conversations and then maybe shop and eat lunch in an establishment which disallows children. We then go home, assemble children and either go out for dinner, buy in a takeaway, heat up a pizza and then argue over who is going to light the candles on the birthday cake. Birthday chocolates will be shared, although some will be retained for later when children are in bed. It is acknowledged that any chocolates which are not consumed that day are in danger of being disappeared by the following evening unless very expertly hidden.

If our children find our own birthdays difficult to cope with, for whatever reason, it is worth exploring this with them. 'I noticed that you found my birthday difficult' and 'I wonder why you found it difficult' might be good places to start. If they've shown challenging behaviours during your birthday then they might be feeling terribly shameful about it. And after all, they didn't set out to ruin your birthday. Likewise, if they've handled a birthday well then let them know (quietly).

Adoption anniversaries

You may choose to mark the anniversary of the day you became a family, or you may not. It is a problematic day to say the least, and as parents we must guard against our own hopes and emotions around that day blinding us to the emotions of our children. For them it is not likely to be an occasion full of joyous memories and associations, but a reminder of loss and a marker of difference. They may not feel able to share this with us either because they are young and don't yet have the ability to recognise and express these painful feelings, or because they don't want to cause us hurt.

These days we hand over the choice of whether we mark the day as a family to our children. This year one ducked out until the last moment and the other was keen to do something. We had a greasy breakfast followed by cycling and lots of fresh air. Over breakfast we briefly recalled the first few days we met and that was it. 'We understand that it is a difficult day for you' was the over-riding theme. I said something corny about how empty and sad my life would be without them, because it's true. I want them to know that despite everything that has happened, they are our number one. We all need to know we are someone's number one.

CHAPTER 4

LEISURE TIME

Play

Before raising our children I had never thought that deeply about play. I knew I liked the word. It sounds like fun. And I knew children (and some adults) do a lot of it and that it is important for their psychological and physical development. That was about as far as I'd got.

Little did I know how much play and playfulness would come to dominate our family life. Our children play all the time, with anything they can lay their hands on and sometimes with things which they are not meant to be able to lay their hands on. We have fed baby dolls and wheeled them around parks, we've blown out plastic birthday candles and handed out plastic pieces of cake on small plastic plates, we've driven cars around mini-car parks, we've enacted motorway pile-ups, we've built and destroyed vast wobbly towers made out of bricks. We've also squoodged dough, poured water, cut up paper, bashed saucepan lids and threaded beads.

The amount of play our children have wanted (and I think needed) has taken me by surprise. It is as though the experiences and learning that come from play just don't stick, or are not trusted and need to be repeated over and over and over. And yes, I know that young children need repetition, but I'm talking about the older years too. They have and continue to fill their boots with play, sometimes calmly and sometimes at great speed and with great purpose.

Often the play has been loaded with metaphor. For one child, everything is about babies and mothers. First it was baby dolls and now it is foals and horses, piglets and pigs, ducks and ducklings, all paired up in neat little pens. This play is pursued with a persistence which I think points to something much deeper than an interest in farm animals. I may be wrong, but it is something which marks us out from families around us.

Likewise, our other child has always been obsessed with emergencies: fire engines, police vans, riot police, car crashes and 'baddies'. We have played out some pretty horrific scenarios in Lego® and Playmobil® over the years. Usually there is a victim and the victim is in peril and must be got to a place of safety. I'm no psychologist but it's not hard to work out where this might be coming from.

I haven't always been too smart at playing with our children in a therapeutic way (that's what exhaustion does to a person), but I am getting there. I've been on a training day with Margot Sunderland, who is a child and adult psychotherapist, writer and generally clever and insightful woman, and she has opened my eyes to the value and the meaning of the play I've been witnessing and taking part in for all this time. After listening to Margot though, I realised that some of the play I'd initiated was therapeutic in nature, even though I hadn't made the connection at the time. For example, I used to get infuriated that despite the numbers of boxes of plasters and bandages I bought, the first aid cupboard was always empty when I needed something. Everything in it just disappeared. Sometimes I'd come across a secret stash of plaster packets. Approaching it head on (nagging, threatening) made no difference at all so I went in the other direction and bought a bag full of cheap plasters and bandages and we played A&E nurses and patients and Vet Clinic for hours and hours. And guess what? It worked. I've since used the same strategy with soap, shampoo and bubble bath. I think that sometimes our children try really hard to communicate their needs to us and when it takes ages for the penny to drop (as it did with me) they up the behaviours until it does.

Even in these teenage years I spot opportunities for working through issues by employing playfulness, whether that's through music lyrics, film, drawings or whatever. We watch an awful lot of fly-on-the-wall emergency and animal rescue documentaries on the television which are a rich source of discussion. I used to think that the window for exploring issues through playfulness was quite small, but now I've changed my mind.

I know our family has been lucky that despite past traumas, our children have wanted and felt able to engage in play. There are many adopted children who find it hard to lose themselves in alternative worlds and engage with others on a playful level. I've learned that play isn't always what we traditionally label it as. Play can be kicking a ball around, cooking, digging in the dirt, sharing a story or colouring in a picture. The book *Creating Loving Attachments* by Kim Golding and Daniel Hughes, apart from being a great and readable guide, has a useful section on play which has helped me to remember the importance of play when I'm flagging a bit. I recommend it particularly for those parents whose children find it difficult to engage in play.

When times are hard and we are stressed to the eyeballs, getting on the floor and driving a bin lorry in and out of a rubbish tip of screwed up newspaper, for an hour-and-a-half isn't exactly what we might feel like doing. As with lots of aspects of adoptive parenting, the amount and quality of play we do with our children can be a massive source of jangling guilt. We don't do enough. We do it too begrudgingly. We can't keep focused. We allow ourselves to become frustrated and disengaged. We find it boring. If only we were more creative. I have beaten myself over the head with all of the above. The truth is, playing with young children, particularly those with attachment difficulties, can be tedious, boring, frustrating and enraging. Adding siblings into the mix, who take any hint that their brother or sister is getting more attention than they are, can multiply all these reactions by a factor of five. Sometimes just hearing the words, 'Why aren't you playing with me?' is enough to send us running to the nearest corner. The conclusion I've come to is that it's better to play when we really feel the joy of it, than to force ourselves to endure it and ooze irritation. It is fine to say, 'I am doing something else for a while but I am looking forward to playing with you later.' Playing with a bored and irritable adult is not great for our children.

When I feel tempted to give in to the 'If only I'd played with them more then this, that or the other behaviour would be a whole lot better' voice in my head, I look through our photographs and our films and remind myself that over the years I have taken part in, initiated, led and been led by hours and hours and hours of play. On balance I think I did the best I could.

Now they are older, play has for our children become more of a private pastime and there is a certain embarrassment around it. It might be that their peers are no longer playing in the same way and it is seen as 'babyish'. There are worries over what might happen if friends find out they are still playing with certain toys. A while ago I was becoming exercised that our oldest child was playing with toys meant for younger children and encouraged him to put them in the loft. Even though I knew that he needed to play, I still found myself discouraging it. What an idiot. Luckily our social worker helped me to see sense. 'What is it you want?' she asked me, 'sexualised behaviours, drug-taking, drinking, hanging around on street corners? Because that's the other extreme and I see plenty of that.' It was the wake-up call I needed. I apologised to our son, got his toys down from the loft and explained that his brain needed to play in order to continue to develop. Now we're at the stage when he will happily play when he wants to and yet tell me when he wants his toys hidden away from friends. These days our children don't want me to interfere in their imaginary play worlds very often, but we still do plenty of other forms of play together like cooking, drawing and other more 'grown-up' pursuits. If I'm entirely honest, I much prefer this type of play.

Snakes and ladders

'Competitive games are good for children because they learn to win with grace and lose with valour' say people with no experience of raising traumatised children. Yet if you want a short route to a long meltdown in many adoptive homes, suggesting everyone plays a competitive game is a sure way of achieving that. To a child who believes themselves to be bad, being moments from success only to slide down a very long snake into inevitable loss can be too much to take. Likewise landing on Mayfair, on which their brother has developed three luxury hotels, is enough to bring all those mixed feelings of sibling rivalry to the surface, all on the throw of a dice. 'You have lost because you are rubbish' is the only lesson they learn. Games are not simply a merry diversion for traumatised children; they are symbolic of life and will either confirm what they already know to be true about themselves (snake) or conflict with it (ladder). If children cannot cope with playing such 'character-building' games then shut them away (the games) in a cupboard for a while. Competitive games are not the be all and end all.

We have had some success with games where there are little wins along the way such as 'Yahtzee' and some of the Orchard games like 'Spotty Dogs' and 'Pop to the Shops' where the fun is had in the spinning of the wheel or the popping to the shops and not really in the winning. We've also developed some simple versions of card games that are quick to play and based mainly on chance. 'Happy Families' has been popular (and comes with its own amusing dash of irony for the grown-ups). Our big breakthrough came when we played a card game called 'Bingo' every evening during a holiday. We bought a big box of chocolates and after every round, everyone got one, whether they'd won or lost. The desire for chocolate trumped the desire to win. These little forays into game-playing have helped to build resilience over the years and now we can play some more directly competitive games, when everyone is in the right mood (though not very often).

Some parents, who are better people than me, advise that we must allow our children to win games. I am not very good at losing on purpose. In fact, I am terrible at it and I would go so far as to admit it is a character flaw. I am much better at pretending I am losing and then going in for a sudden and devastating victory. This is unforgiveable behaviour as a therapeutic parent. What I am better at is really hamming it up when I've lost. Oh how I cry and wail and complain. 'Mum is such a terrible loser' someone will say and then I'll be counselled by a child about why winning isn't all that important. It's kind of therapeutic parenting in reverse and it is fun too. This approach only works when I feel like it though, and when no one is wavering on the precipice of a meltdown or they will think I am taking the piss (which I sort of am). What children often can't cope with is over-egged praise when they win. We instinctively feel that we want to make a big deal of them winning, but even this can push them over.

It can be difficult to close the door on the games cupboard when all around you are extolling the importance of games. You may start to worry that your child is going to miss valuable educational lessons, fall behind, get an E in GCSE Maths, be unemployed for the rest of their lives. Rest assured, they won't face a life of unemployment because you haven't forced them to play 'Mousetrap'.

Sports

Like so many aspects of life, sport is something that adoptive families have to think about from first principles. We can't fall into the pitfalls of going along with generally accepted norms like 'sport is good for all children' or 'team games teach essential skills'. Putting a child whose head is full of fear, chaos and noise in the middle of a football pitch and have other children shout at them 'shoot for god's sake' might not be a great idea. Putting a child who is terrified of rough physical contact in the middle of a rugby pitch definitely isn't. I have a sporty child, who has amazing hand–eye and hand–foot coordination. He could drop-kick a rugby ball at the age of three and wallop a tennis ball with a cricket bat at the age of four. To all intents and purposes he is a natural for the football and the rugby pitch. Unfortunately his ability to cope with being surrounded by other children, with multiple instructions, or with planning a strategy, has been severely impaired, and this causes him to freeze. He stood in the middle of one competitive football match, the ball coming towards him and watched an airplane fly overhead, as his 'team mates' shouted at him in disbelief. He would love to play football and be part of the gang and not being able to makes him feel like a loser. I could cry for him. A history of neglect and abuse robs children of many possible futures.

I know children with similar early experiences who are very good at contact sports and who benefit greatly from being part of a team and having the opportunity to release energy during training and matches. There are no rules.

My own sporty child, I have learned, copes very well with racket sports like tennis and badminton. He likes to play singles so there is no danger he is going to be bumped by other children. He is too shy to join a club so I play with him, not as often as I should, but I do. And he wears his football kit.

Swimming is a major source of competitive parenting and something else that adoptive parents might have to approach differently to everyone else. I don't know if I'm living in some swimming lesson-obsessed part of the country, but for a long time I felt under huge pressure to make both our children endure weekly swimming lessons. Maybe I thought that if I didn't my children would drown in a canal or a quarry or something. The lessons were so over-subscribed that I had to queue to sign up for them at a ridiculously early time in the morning. Twice a week we would stand in a hot, noisy and chaotic changing room waiting to go into the pool, where the children would sit and gaze into the distance and get told off for not concentrating. While one was swimming the other would run around the waiting area, touching and climbing on everything, much to the disgruntlement of the other parents. It was a nightmare and I don't know what I was thinking putting us all through it. The final straw came when our daughter had to be dragged off me by the swimming instructor screaming, 'Don't make me go with the scary fat lady' (dear daughter, I am so sorry I let that happen). I came to my senses and cancelled all lessons. I've since taken them both swimming myself, they've had a few lessons at school and a few during the summer holidays. They will never swim for their country, but they were never going to, and our week is considerably calmer and happier. I've also saved a lot of money which helps with the other hidden costs of being an adoptive parent.

Computer games

One moment our children are playing 'Operation' and decorating fairy cakes, and the next they are wanting to play hideously violent computer games. 'But I can switch the blood off' they say and 'So and so plays that and he's only eight' before losing all control and launching a PE bag at your head. Not long afterwards will come, 'You are the only mum I know who doesn't let her child play Call of Duty.' And they are probably right. For a long time now and as far as I can tell I have stood alone in not allowing my child to play 18-rated games, and frankly I find that disturbing. Even if my children were healthily attached, with no emotional issues at all, I would not let them play 18-rated games. The games are getting more and more violent and misogynistic and I don't know how bad they would have to get before parents say 'enough'.

Children who have experienced violence should definitely not be playing violent computer games in my opinion. It has caused many, many arguments and meltdowns in our family, but I know that I'm making the right decision for our children. Over the past few years I have tried to explain to my son why I don't think that violent games are good for him. We've started to talk about the traumatised brain and how it is affected by images of violence and also about storylines that demean women. We're now able to have some more mature and emotionally literate conversations which have led on to debates about the presentation of women in the pop industry and broader equal rights. I know I made the right call, so if you are feeling isolated and under pressure, take some courage from me. Therapeutic parenting is not always 'doing it differently'; sometimes it's 'doing it better'.

This is something our son wrote about violent games:

> *Other boys talk about violent games which I am not allowed because it makes me more aggressive towards other people. I have played them before in front of my mum and she saw the slitting of throats and we got rid of it and my aggression improved.*

The internet and social networking

I don't entirely buy into the inevitability of social networking and certainly not for children with attachment issues who fall below the legal age limit for sites like Facebook and Twitter. Our children find face-to-face friendships complex and perplexing and friendships are so often the cause of anger and sadness. They can take the smallest sleight, even an imagined sleight, as a shot to the heart, they can overdo things being too clingy or silly, and they miss or misinterpret social cues like facial expressions and body language. Friendships seem an easy, natural thing to make and maintain for those of us who have healthy attachment histories (most of the time anyway). For our children who often function emotionally below their chronological age they are a minefield. Whenever I'm floundering about in new territory I often find myself going back to the old mantra, 'think toddler'. This has been particularly useful when it comes to friendships and social networking.

Facebook is not my personal go-to social network of choice. I dipped into it for a time and found it good in parts but preachy and smug in others. There were too many, 'Look what a marvellous time we're having' and 'Bless my child for getting top marks in all his SATs,' and the 'Like this unless you are some kind of a monster' really got on my wick. I'm glad that I've had some exposure to it, the way it can hijack your emotions for a moment, make you question friendships you feel secure about in reality and waste your time with childish 'like this or else'-type garbage.

It is no wonder that Facebook is such a minefield for children with attachment difficulties. On top of what I struggled with, there is the indignity and shame of being rejected as a friend in black and white; there are playground fallouts played out after school; there is the temptation to respond to something unwisely and emotionally which is then on show.

We stuck to the 'You are not 13 yet' line for as long as we could and then bored our son to death with lectures about the pitfalls of social networking. We set up his account and worked through the security settings together. I have his password and can check when I need to. My sister is a 'friend' and keeps an eye out for anything risky. I have learnt that with any new and potentially risky activity one has to let out the rope slowly and be ready to bring it in a bit if the freedom is too much for them to handle. We have to accept that they will make mistakes but try to ensure that their mistakes are not too catastrophic.

The website www.thinkuknow.co.uk contains lots of advice about keeping children safe on the internet. It contains films which show how adults can impersonate children. It is tempting as parents to put our heads in the sand, but if my experience is anything to go by, if there is the possibility of exposure to risk on the internet, then our children will root it out. I often marvel that children with such clear cognitive difficulties can demonstrate such skill in knocking down safety barriers and accessing risk.

Despite my vigilance, there have been several attempts to open secret social networking accounts. Fortunately they were foiled quickly but could have had serious implications. One such attempt had appeared to attract the attention of some dubious people. This all happened despite us working through the Child Exploitation and Online Protection Centre (CEOP) website together. It isn't a nice thing to put into black and white, but our children can make terrible choices. Because of this we must be vigilant wherever the internet is concerned. You will know what suits your family. Despite our vigilance it can sometimes feel like being under constant cyber-attack.

Children will inevitably become too old and too clever to be contained by our cyber-security and may seek to make contact with birth family members. Indeed unsolicited contact may come back the other way. Either way, sudden and unsolicited contact is very less than desirable, especially coming as it might, during teenage years. I hope that we've done enough therapeutic work and enough life history work to lessen the chances of it happening and the fallout if it does. Our collective adoption stories all contain many shock storylines and unexpected events. Perhaps I'm taking too much the head in the sand approach, but I'll do everything I can to prevent unsolicited contact (and I'm not the Thames barrier). And if I worried about everything that could go wrong, I wouldn't sleep.

'*Please* can we get a dog?'

'*Please* can we get a dog?' or its more upfront relation, 'When are we getting a dog?' are sentences I never want to hear again in my life. In fact I don't even want to hear the words 'dog', 'puppy' or 'kitten'. We are not getting a dog or a puppy or a kitten and that's the end of it.

It appears to be common for children with histories of neglect to like animals, either that or I just happen to have been around a lot of them. I use the word 'like' but what I really mean is 'be completely obsessed with'. And how lovely it is, to get them a little four-legged something to take care of and love and nurture. The only problem is, traumatised children can be horrid to animals. They don't mean to be.

I've watched children who just don't understand how to be with animals. They go at them, corner them, touch them too much and too hard, don't notice the flicking tail, or the change in the stance or the mew or bark or whatever it is. They might get a bite and a scratch which will upset them terribly and then within a moment are back for more. There are also reports of children abusing animals in the way they themselves have been abused. For these reasons I think it is wise to be cautious when thinking about having pets in an adoptive household.

I was nagged and nagged and nagged about getting a pet, until I was so mentally exhausted I almost forgot my own name. (That's another special talent which many traumatised children seem to have in common.) We ended up with a rescue cat called Ron. Ron was starving hungry all the time and scared of humans. She spent much of the first few weeks in our home on top of the fridge freezer. She was pursued relentlessly by both children who competed with each other for cat-related contact. It was horrendous. Things are better now, five years on, but I still find myself saying on a daily basis, 'Leave the cat alone' and have to make sure Ron hasn't been trapped in a room somewhere.

Luckily Ron the cat has become an excellent therapeutic pet and takes her self-care very seriously, but I feel guilty over what she was put through. We should have realised that our children would fight over her and not be able to leave her alone when she needed it and actually were not ready for a pet. And her presence added a lot of stress into our home when we really didn't need it. Luckily our children have never lashed out and hurt her, but I know of households where this has happened. The pet has been in the wrong place at the wrong time and been on the sharp end of an angry outburst.

I would never suggest 'don't have pets' at all because all our families are different. A lot depends of course on what our children can cope with and their trauma history. I'm just saying think hard about it and consider waiting until maturity is on its way. Think particularly hard about what you can manage. Some of us with challenging family lives may at times feel on the verge of collapse and the additional responsibility that comes with having a pet may just be enough to tip us over.

I am still to this day being mentally tortured because I refuse to give in to having a dog. Every single day I am pleaded with and bullied. If we leave the house we have to stroke every single dog that crosses our path, for so long that the owner gets pissed off. We watch every TV programme there is about dogs, we have dog encyclopaedias, toy dogs with collars and beds, we look at dog rescue websites and monitor the price of various breeds in the newspaper. Whenever I feel myself wavering I remind myself of my elite parent status. Everyone else can have a dog because they are regular parents. I'm running a different race here.

Having a laugh

Laughter (and sometimes near hysteria) has eased Mr D. and me through the difficulties of the past few years. Fortunately we both have a similar sense of humour and can find the funny even in the smelliest, darkest, dankest of places. Oh how we've laughed. We've laughed mainly as we've looked back on things (the present has not always been an easy source of comedy). From a distance there is a certain amusement to be found in the games of noughts and crosses played out in biro on the new jeans, the water in my face cream, the nail varnish decorating the bathroom tiles, the scissor cuts in the towels, the pretence of eating breakfast (by careful arrangement of a bowl with a splash of milk in and a lone Shreddie), the pretence of cleaning teeth, the getting up 25 times a night for a 'wee', the shock of being called 'a paedophile' in front of our neighbour. I could go on. And on. And on.

There is something about the extremity of the lives of therapeutic parents which if it weren't funny might be close to unbearable. For me, the laughing, when it starts, is sometimes unstoppable and can end in tears of I'm not sure quite what. Unfortunately, my release valve tends to get activated at the most inopportune moments, like when I see an old lady fall over in the street, or my husband suffers a terribly painful back spasm. I am overcome by a flood of everything which has been stored up and rendered helpless and hysterical and fighting for breath. 'It wasn't that funny' is something I hear quite a lot.

Traumatised children can drag the extremes of emotion out of us, including mirth. There's nothing as therapeutic as a laugh so hearty it grips you by the guts and won't let go, particularly if it is shared.

Humour has got our family through some dark times, greased the wheels, defused a few hand-grenades and released pressure that might otherwise have spilled out in destructive ways. Laughing together creates a special sharing experience, a bond. Whenever I laugh uncontrollably and one of my children catches the laughter, as they laugh they look deep into my eyes in a way that they never do otherwise and like the brain doctors say, our brains sort of reach out and touch each other.

When trauma behaviours are engulfing our families it is a hard ask to remember to laugh and it is not always appropriate. Humour, though, is not a fussy customer; it can be found virtually anywhere. It is there in the shit, the refusals, the banging and the crashing, the swearing and the stamping, but it can take time to feel safe enough to come out.

Inappropriately timed humour, aimed at our children, as many of us have learned to our cost, can be like throwing a can of petrol into a bonfire. It is because we haven't understood. Our child is saying, 'I need a warm jumper' and we've thrown them a whoopee cushion. We've not taken them seriously and they will rage until we do.

It is important, no matter how angry we are feeling, to find opportunities to laugh. Children can sense a safety around adults who laugh. When I ask my children which teachers they particularly like they will both reply with a few names and the reason they like them is 'Because they are really funny, but also a bit strict.' They enjoy a joke but they still need to know that things are under control. Of course there is no magic potion which will get everyone laughing, but a few things work for us: the comedy series 'Malcolm in the Middle', 'The Simpsons', 'You've Been Framed' and YouTube videos which involve people slipping around on ice. Making the decision to go and see a funny film or doing anything to lighten a tense and unhappy atmosphere can take some resolve (especially if there are lingering feelings that a child needs to be punished and not rewarded for some misdemeanour or other) but it can change the mood music and the narrative of the day or the weekend. Laughing is therapy for all the family, and cheaper and more available than family therapy. One Christmas Eve, in a state of high stress I took our children out for one of my unplanned and inevitably disastrous walks. I know not how but we found ourselves climbing a ridiculously steep and muddy hill. The children were small. The hill was so steep that we couldn't get any traction at all and had to grab at spindly branches and shoots to avoid sliding all the way back down again. I was piggy backed by a tiny mud-covered child who was laughing, the other was falling and sliding and laughing and laughing. The situation I had got us into was ridiculous and the laughter was infectious. It was brilliant. So I would say, no matter how grim things feel, go and find some fun.

One area of humour which, in my experience, definitely does not work with traumatised children is sarcasm. Sarcasm can work between one healthily attached person and another, as long as it is carefully constructed and aimed. If my friend says to me, 'You're looking gross today' I know that she is saying I look good today because I have a basic belief that I am not gross and because her body language and facial expressions tell me she is trying (not altogether successfully) to be funny. We have also established friendship and trust over a long period and implicitly understand the ground rules upon which our relationship is based. There can be disastrous consequences from using sarcasm with our children. They believe, in fact they know, that they are gross and they find non-verbal communication difficult to interpret, therefore they will take 'You're looking particularly gross today' literally and as an arrow through the heart. Once they have taken offence it is pointless bleating, 'I meant it as a joke.'

A few years ago I was chatting to an adopter during a break in a training course who was incensed that her son just couldn't get her sarcasm. I got and enjoyed her sarcasm. She explained that a sarcastic statement such as, 'Come on ugly bug' or 'Can't you get your handwriting any messier?' would result in him raging and 'ruining the day for everyone'. In her view (as a healthy, well-attached individual) he must toughen up and accept such statements as 'jokes'. I tried the whole 'but perhaps to him they are not jokes but poke at the pain of his truth' and didn't get anywhere. She was in the place perhaps where she wanted him fixed and was not as yet prepared to compromise. I liked her and found her very funny, and meeting her reminded me of how very flexible we must be in our thinking if we are to provide a safe space for our children. I've no doubt that some of her frustration was not that he couldn't 'get' her humour but that the smallest things can derail a day and I get that. Sarcasm, if it is an integral part of us, can be hard to give up. We might want to hang on to it hard as though in letting go of it we might be letting a bit of ourselves go.

As our children become comfortable with us and begin to really trust us I have found that some gentle sarcasm can be introduced into the orchestra, especially directed towards a third person who you know will find it funny, or to an absent person who deserves it.

'Today a boy at school told me that I've got a big ugly nose and my hair is shit.'

'What's his name? Harry Styles?'

This is perfectly acceptable I think because it is empathetic in nature, allowing our child to share in the joke whilst also helping them to develop effective retorts.

'A boy at school said to me, "Your mum's an undateable."'

'How did that make you feel?'

'I was very angry that he called you that.'

'Please tell him I should very much like to meet him next time I come into school, he sounds delightful.'

This is also acceptable. We use this type of scenario quite often and it allows us to dissipate at least some of the pain with some laughter.

Used with care, sarcasm can be employed to approach minor behaviours, but only once that behaviour has been named and explored over time. In our house a minor school uniform indiscretion is a small but clear sign that the wearer is looking for a confrontation. Sometimes it can lead to greater and greater indiscretions until there is refusal to conform to almost all rules. So whilst it usually needs to be nipped in the bud, there is also a danger that in pointing out the indiscretion, the desired confrontation is enabled. Depending on the prevailing mood (mine as well as the child's) I will either ignore the green socks and tackle them another time, or say something like:

'I see it's a green sock day today. Do I need to run for cover?'

Or if I'm in proper therapeutic parenting mode, which I might not be five minutes before the school bus is about to leave:

'Ah green socks. Is there something you're trying to tell me?'

On reflection, that one might be better kept for when the school bus returns in the afternoon.

Family traditions

Aside from the traditions which are forced upon us by way of culture or religion, all families have their own traditions which have developed organically and naturally. Their origins may be lost in the mists of time. These family traditions connect us together in mutual enjoyment and bonding. They remind us we are part of an exclusive tribe with experiences that are shared and appreciated amongst the 'in-crowd'. It is important for our children to feel part of the 'in-crowd' I think. In so many other parts of their lives they experience the cold shoulder of the 'out-crowd'.

An important part of family traditions in our household are 'in jokes'. 'In jokes' can grow out of all sorts of common experiences. Some may be based around funny words or expressions that our children used as they learned to talk. 'Mermermaid' my daughter used to say around the time she was filling her boots with Tinkerbell. So mermaids will forever be known as 'mermermaids' in our family, or sometimes even 'mermermermermaids'.

Traditions don't have to be hard and fast but may be temporary. One child likes to watch the BBC wildlife programme *Spring Watch* with me. We must sit on the sofa together, under a blanket. The getting out of the blanket and the arranging of the event is as much as part of it as the watching. For the time that programme is on air we have that experience in common, we discuss the progress of the baby owls, the nesting habits of the water birds. Although the experience itself lasts for a few weeks a year our bonding memories will never go away. I hope that in years to come when our daughter is reminiscing with friends about watching *Spring Watch* she will remember those shared moments of nurture and love with me.

Traditions can grow out of almost anything; a song that everyone particularly likes, a film, a place. There may be traditions around holidays. My mum used to make a giant boiled fruitcake for our annual caravan holidays to the south coast of England. Every evening as the sun set on a busy day on the beach my mum, my dad, my sister and me would sit around the caravan table and eat fruitcake and drink hot chocolate and play card games. It was a treat, it was fun and it gave the end of the day some rhythm, comfort and loose structure. This is what we are aiming to cloak our children in.

When I reflect on some of my own adoptive family's traditions they are somehow different to my childhood family traditions. I couldn't reliably get everyone through a day on holiday in a stable enough mood to want to sit around and eat cake in the evening. We do have certain games we play, but this wouldn't happen every night. Going back for a moment to the musical analogy, my children demand a lot more improvisation than me and my sister did, they are much more unpredictable and less likely to fall in with what everyone else wants to do. The rhythms must be more adaptable. And the cake itself would become an object of fantasy and obsession, it would be sneakily picked at and repeatedly asked about. I think I would end up hating the cake.

When all is dark and we feel like folding in on ourselves it is difficult to reach above the mayhem and jangled nerves for the restorative arms of family tradition, but it is worth it. It demonstrates to children with a fractured sense of belonging that whatever they have done or said, no matter how angry everyone has got, family traditions will be there as a demonstration of unconditional love. I have referred before to our own family tradition of having sweets on a Friday. The sweets are given no matter what has happened during the week and are known as 'Friday Sweets'. It is worthwhile thinking about your own family traditions. Maybe they will be able to help you through some difficult times.

CHAPTER 5

REPETITIVE STRAIN

Learning the hard way

During times of stress, you may find yourself saying (as you run your fingers through your hair in quiet desperation) 'Why do you always have to learn things the hard way?' I certainly have. It's not a terribly therapeutic response, I admit, but I am not some kind of bloodless Therabot. My unreconstructed, untherapeutic reactions sometimes (often) leak out. Occasionally, hidden within these outbursts are gems of truth.

Our children seem to have to learn from repeated and direct experience (the hard way). Not your experience or mine, or their friend's, or their brother's, or the children's on the infomercial. No, they must try everything. First-hand experience is the only experience that matters, and even that has to be retested and retested. I sometimes wonder if this is something unique to my own family but then I see it in other adoptive families too and you may see it in yours.

How I've managed to prevent our youngest child from falling foul of a hideous accident in the home, or out in the street, is a miracle I will always be thankful for and never fully understand. As a younger child she was magnetically attracted to sharp edges, concrete steps, big drops, hot things, stinging things and biting things. During a winter walk along a particularly badly worn track near our house, I said to her, 'Don't go into that puddle, it is deeper than you are.' She immediately jumped into the puddle (and was marched home, in sub-zero temperatures, covered in dark brown, smelly sludge). She didn't only do it once. Even last week she attempted to *cycle* through it. As they get older the lessons become more complex and higher risk and harder to learn. The only method I've found which makes any ounce of difference is speak out loud what I think may be about to happen, before it does, and then to spell out the choices.

I might say, 'I'm about to bring a hot dish to the table and I'm guessing that you are going to find it difficult not to touch it, so I'm just warning you that if you do then you may burn your finger, oh you did, that must hurt, oh dear.' Only a few weeks ago, I had to intervene as our children found themselves physically fighting over a kettle of boiling water. And lest anyone feels tempted to advise me that all children do this, I'm talking about children of a double-digit age here. With smaller children we can choose to avoid situations altogether and not bring the dish to the table, or we can hide away the knives, the matches, the razors, the medicine on a high shelf. With older children, it's not always that easy. When they can look you in the eye it is virtually impossible to squirrel things away in high places. I do, however, have a few sneaky low hiding places, which no one has discovered (yet).

Electronic devices and passcodes have been another source of repetitive strain in our house. 'I've set your passcode as your birthday, I wouldn't change it if I were you' I say into the wind. I've been back to the O2 shop to get the mobile phone reset FOUR TIMES. Mr D. has had to reload the iPod for the same reason THREE TIMES.

There are occasions when the thinking involved has to be a little more predictive. I know that around school disco time there will be an overwhelming desire to (a) take cash from my purse and (b) decorate the bathroom with nail varnish. I do my best to hide my purse and the nail varnish, say that they have been hidden and the reason why (to avoid temptation) and that they will be presented in good time. This is known as Heading Off the Armies of Chaos at Think Ahead Pass.

It is tempting, when a particular behaviour hasn't been present for a while, to forget about it and hope it's gone away, as though by mentioning it we may somehow jinx it back to life. I'm sure I don't need to tell you what a mistake that strategy is. It is always worth remembering to say, 'I've noticed you've been doing really well at not annoying the cat/playing with the nail varnish/cutting up the soap, well done.' If your children are anything like mine they will try to shake off even that small amount of praise as quickly as possible. But drop it in anyway, in fuss-free small amounts. Some of it sticks, I'm sure of that. And even if the behaviour makes a return, it will be its last death rattle.

Some of the repetitive failing is utterly out of our children's control. I'm thinking about the times when they become over-excited, or overcome by pressure or emotions. I'm thinking of the child who is looking forward to having a friend over to play so much that he then can't relax with the friend and it ends in tears. For these sorts of repetitive 'failures' (although I don't really like that word) our children need to be supported in order that the event is a success. Something along the lines of, 'You know how you really look forward to Billy coming over and then when you play together you get so, so excited or angry and sometimes hit him with a toy or something? You don't? Alright then, but I was thinking that if it looks like that might happen, which it probably won't, then I'll sit with you/join in with the game/take you for some fresh air.' This recognises that our child may not yet be ready or able to learn from mistakes and need help (and it demonstrates acceptance and empathy).

I can't deny that all this forward thinking, planning ahead and strategising is easy. It isn't. It is like the longest, most complicated, most draining game of chess ever. See, I told you this was elite parenting.

A lack of cause and effect thinking is at the heart of many challenges faced in our family. Our children can act in an instant, not planning, weighing up, measuring, or calculating. They may tell you to f**k off one moment and then be completely surprised that you then don't want to laugh with them during a mealtime five minutes later, or immediately top up their mobile phone for them. In fact it comes as a total shock to them that there is any connection between them telling you to f**k off and your subsequent human reaction. As small children, how often, when you say, 'If you do that again then such and such will happen' do they immediately go and do that thing again? Their lack of cause and effect thinking means that we have to do quite a lot of it for them until they are able to start doing it for themselves.

Some experts make a big thing of lack of cause and effect thinking, and wonder if it indicates other more medicalised diagnoses. Maybe it does. I don't know. But I've noticed an awful lot of it in adopted children. And there is that small matter of the impact of early trauma on the developing brain, particularly the parts responsible for cognitive thinking such as planning ahead and predicting outcomes. That, teamed with impulsivity and needing to maintain control at all times, makes for a heady cocktail. The truth is, our children need us alongside them, to help them make sense of the world.

It is of course important to remain calm in the face of repeated mistakes. It is also very, very hard. Sure as a bumpy road wears down a bicycle tyre, so our fortitude and patience is worn away. It is a war of attrition, which we must win, but which comes with casualties. Some experts say things like 'Never ever lose your cool,' 'Always be calm' and 'Never lose your temper.' 'Never ever shout' is another. I have sat in training courses where this is the dominant message, gazed up at a bar set so high I knew I had no hope of ever reaching it and wondered what on earth was wrong with me that I couldn't just follow these simple rules. I would drive home feeling terribly guilty, resolve never ever to shout again, shout again and then feel like a horrible, unfit, monster of a mother. I have broken every single one of these rules, many, many times over, and I think it's important to feel able to say that. I have broken them because I am, like you, human and therefore fallible, particularly under extreme and extended mind-blowing pressure (pressure which many people without experience of parenting traumatised, emotionally damaged children have little appreciation of).

Our child will see us losing our cool and getting frustrated with them and this sends them into shame and self-loathing, so we must limit as far as possible the times the mask of calm and control slips. But to expect ourselves to never slip up is, I think, unrealistic. Slipping up occasionally is part of being human and part of our humanity. So, too, is cooling down and apologising. Even if it were possible, I'm not sure about the rightness of modelling only calm and control to our children. If they don't witness the full rainbow of emotions in us, I wonder how they become able to accept their own anger, sadness and frustration. I'm not saying we should become raging furnaces of uncontrolled feeling, but that if our children sometimes get a glimpse and witness our own coping mechanisms and repair processes in action, then that might not be a bad thing.

My own children are starting to make good headway in predictive thinking and working out the natural consequences of their actions, so part of this I report from the other side. There is hope. I have, however, spent many years doing the predictive thinking for them. It's like being the plastercast supporting a broken bone. Eventually that bone starts to knit together and gain strength and bits of the plastercast can be removed and replaced with a crepe bandage.

There are times when I have found it useful and effective to nurture predictive thinking skills by thinking through consequences together in a clear and logical way. At a decision point, when things are rocking along and I notice that a child is in danger of making a terrible 'choice', I call a temporary halt and we all take a breath. 'At this point you could do A' I might say, 'or you could do B'. 'What might happen if you do A?' I will posit. 'And what might happen if you do B?' The answers are nearly always completely obvious. When children are still running unthinkingly into trouble, they may well be able to pass the A or B test with flying colours and then run off and still make the wrong choice. This is because they are still acquiring the skills to make good choices and are acting upon impulse or in a survival-driven manner. Try not to say 'I can't believe you went and did B right after we agreed A was the right choice' but instead empathise with them. Tell them you know how hard it is for them. And then repeat the exercise at the next decision point and gently remind them about what happened last time and how upset it had made them. This process, I must now tell you, takes years and years before any real improvement takes place. But when they start to get it, big pieces of the puzzle will start to fall into place and you will realise that what you have taught them is a valuable thinking strategy.

'Can't be bothered'

'No, I can't be a***d,' 'It's too boring,' 'There's no point' are all alternative ways of saying 'I am stupid and I am going to fail so I am not going to try it.' The 'it' might be learning a musical instrument, sport, doing a piece of homework or indeed anything which requires practice and a leap of faith. Those of us who are emotionally healthy may not have to think twice before embarking on a new hobby, writing a letter to a friend, attempting to cook a dish we've never cooked before. We have an innate trust and belief in our own capacity to follow instructions, to experiment, and to learn from our mistakes. We believe we are basically good, we trust our experience and talents and forgive ourselves our mistakes.

Many of our children know themselves to be untalented, unskilled, bound to fail and make embarrassing mistakes. Their failures are an outward demonstration of their 'badness'. On the other hand, getting something right risks overturning their world view which is a painful thing to happen. Why would they ever expose themselves in such a brutal way?

Gently encouraging our children to recognise their skills and talents takes bucket loads of time and patience. Helping them to learn that making mistakes is human and nothing to be ashamed of takes oceans of it. If the self-loathing and self-doubt is coupled with a short fuse and a hair trigger temper as it so often is, then practising a skill, let alone learning a new one, can be virtually impossible. Imagine trying to learn a new skill, like perhaps juggling, and a voice says over and over into your ear, 'You are rubbish at this, you're going to drop the ball, ha I told you and you've done it again, you're rubbish,' well that's what I imagine it must feel like.

Homework is the most obvious manifestation of 'can't be bothered' but there is a more heart-breaking impact which prevents our children from accessing life-enhancing hobbies and activities, things which draw us towards like-minded people and soothe the bad times and help us to relax. I've heard adoptive parents say, 'But he has no interests at all' and I can identify with that. A chronic lack of self-belief can be a barrier to our children accessing that which may help them to be less socially isolated and to lead more enriched lives. As I said earlier, trauma robs children of possible futures.

Hobbies and interests come in the end, but slowly and gradually for our children. Small signs of an interest need to be carefully (and not over-bearingly) nurtured because they can be easily snuffed out. And perhaps the marvellous things we see our friend's children doing will always be too much of a stretch for our children who are loaded down with missed development. We are playing a long and finely-balanced game here and we must keep the faith.

Of course all children are different. Perhaps yours are marvellous at playing the oboe or they are the cricket team's best batsman. We are quite good at cooking and lighting fires, and I'm happy with that.

'Where is my other trainer?'

Disorganisation comes with the territory. It's probably fair to say that for most children, being organised and planning ahead is not at the top of their list of priorities, but in our family we take this to a bit of an extreme. It can be amusing to talk about but sometimes it just isn't. And it's the topic that will get the 'all children are like that' pokers and preachers animated. What I'm talking about here is disorganisation on an entirely different scale and level of intensity.

So first I want to say that if you are swimming against a tide of chaos, then I really do understand. On top of everything else, disorganisation can be the last straw. Our children mostly can't help being disorganised and chaotic, but that doesn't make it any easier to deal with. Acting as the imperfect firewall which holds back chaos is tooth-grindingly hard work and I often find myself descending into naggery. I'm not going to riff on all the examples of chaos I could give but I will share with you a few things that have helped to hold it back. Nothing has made a radical difference. As always it's slowly, carefully, relentlessly, patiently does it. And as always we have to be the plastercast and the safety net until our children have the mental space and capacity to start to learn to organise parts of their own lives for themselves.

It's costly, but I buy lots of pairs of school trousers and jumpers. I hear of families who can operate with two of each and can only marvel. The chance of us leaving the house on time in the morning, in a calm fashion, is greatly increased by the procurement of a large quantity of items of school uniform. I call this the trouser:success ratio.

I am also the keeper of a drawer of cheap and frankly terrible quality stationery. When a child presents a pencil case of shards and sharpenings (a common occurrence) I can have it refreshed in no time and with minimum emotion and naggery.

I long ago gave up on the multi-compartmented, colourful lunchbox and matching drink set. They are lovely but lovely things make me cross when they get lost or broken, so for now, the less plastic loveliness in our lives the better it is for everyone. My top tip is the lunchbox-sized ice cream container, or failing that, a roll of plastic bags. That way, no tears are spilt and there will always be something to put a sandwich and a packet of Hula Hoops in. For drinks my husband brings home small cola bottles from work which I wash out. Again, if the emotion is taken out of the losing of the lunchbox/drinking bottle combo then we have more chance of keeping on an even keel.

There are some household items which, if I can't put my hands on, can really, really screw up my day. I'm thinking of things like nail scissors, rechargeable batteries, Sellotape, hair brush, tweezers, soap, hair gel. I now have two of each of these items, and I keep them somewhere secret. I know how I may be sounding, but when a morning has involved trying to locate a single shoe, half a bus pass and then I've been called a fat something or other, I really want to be able to brush my hair with something which hasn't already been used on the cat.

Nagging is not the best way of nurturing a little brain, which is why I think planning for failure is the best and only other option out there. The calmer we can make the home environment, the more relaxed our children will be and the greater the chance that their brains will start to repair and develop. Keeping a drawer full of pens isn't brain science, but actually it kind of is.

Of course we have to try to gently teach our children ways of being organised and prepared. We can stick timetables on the fridge, prompts on the front door, messages on the pin board. If these work for you then use them; if they don't, then don't worry, find something which does, or don't. It's perfectly acceptable to act as a safety net until our children are ready to be a bit more organised. This is the approach I'm going for and we are getting there, slowly but surely.

Regression

Missing out on nurture, attachment to a parent, play, storytelling and other important experiences in early life means that many of our children have generally fallen behind their peers. They can come across as particularly 'immature' and babyish, particularly when they (and you) are under stress. The timing can sometimes be 'challenging'. Baby voices, baby body language, babyish walking, talking and clapping can indicate that our child is back in a more vulnerable place. Their behaviours are screaming, 'I'm not a threat, please don't hurt me.' They learnt the connection between 'cute' behaviour and keeping safe very early on, which is tragic. If you struggle with 'cute' (as I do), then it is useful to try to think about where it is coming from. I've had to really work on the empathy with this one.

I used to get irritated, stressed and embarrassed when our children were behaving in a certain way, not being all grown-up and sensible, not behaving 'age-appropriately'. Whilst I knew I was being unfair and their behaviours were entirely healthy and appropriate considering their past, I still screamed inwardly when a large child ran at me in a supermarket in the manner of a toddler, saying 'me want' rather than 'I want' and then tripping over on purpose. I may even on occasion have muttered, 'For goodness sake act your age.' I know. Monstrous. There is something deep inside me which finds the baby act really disconcerting. I rather reluctantly share this with you in case you feel the same (not so that you can berate me for being an insensitive old witch). I've got over it, partly because the behaviours have diminished and partly because I now give much less of a shit what other people think. Not giving a shit has been of great benefit to me and mine, although if you see me out and about wearing slippers and a onesie, or some such other inappropriate clothing, then please do tell me that not giving a shit has gone a little too far.

Although I have been irritated by what I should probably refer to as something more politically correct like 'delayed behaviours', I was a she-wolf ready to defend my young cubs when I heard it voiced by others. At school I once heard, 'He's very immature compared to the other children in his year and it might start to irritate staff.' Well we can't have that can we? Irritate staff, who only see him for a maximum of an hour a day? Boy I was cross (even though I felt the same), and I set out to scatter some empathy around the staff room.

As our children grow up they may be open to learning about why they are a bit behind their peers in certain respects. I think it is worth explaining that they missed out on a lot when they were babies and are catching up. It's not a difficult concept, and in my experience lowers shame and anxiety and gives hope. Here is something which my son wrote:

> *Because I missed playing when I was younger I'm just catching up and play instead of watching football like everyone else. It makes me calm when I play and I play in my room where no one can disturb me.*

When regressive behaviours appear out of nowhere they are a strong indicator of anxiety in my experience. It is a good time to keep our child close, to be extra playful with them and to try to understand what it is that's unnerved them. Usually it is obvious and we need to empathise with their anxieties. Something like, 'I wonder if you're feeling a bit worried about the school trip on Friday' is a good opener. 'I get a bit worried if I have to go somewhere I've never been before' is also an approach which works well in our house. 'It makes me feel funny in my tummy' can help to depersonalise and depressurise the issue. Often just voicing it can help, even if the child doesn't acknowledge, or even denies it.

When you think you have got close to working out whatever is causing the anxiety then you can come up with strategies to help. In the example I've given, I would inform the school so that they can deal with the situation with empathy; I might give my child something of mine to take on the trip; or if they were really troubled by the trip I might go on it myself, or (and I must whisper this) keep them off school for the day. It is not, in my opinion, worth forcing a child to go on a trip if it is going to cause them huge anxiety. There may be longer-term regressions at times of transition and change, for example, when changing classes, or moving up to the next stage in education. These situations need to be planned for well in advance.

Our children may at times want to engage us in baby play. They may want to be fed like a baby, rocked and pretend to have their nappy changed. I played with my child in this way for hours and hours. He led the play and it was as though he couldn't get enough of it. He needed the intimacy, the repetition and the relaxation I think. And it wasn't just a one-way street. As we played at mother and baby, we smelt each other and touched each other and bonded. I hope it created some better memories for him of being babied. I must just mention that it can feel a bit weird playing babies with a child who is not a baby. I had moments of what I can only describe as 'queasiness' for which I blame certain Channel 5 documentaries featuring big blokes wearing nappies and giant babygros. My approach was to pull back a bit if I really felt odd and refocus. It is not our nurture-starved child's fault that modern culture has lodged these images into our minds.

Babying, cuddling, rocking, being close and playing hand-clapping games are all like magic gold dust in terms of healing our interrupted children. If we are able to, we should give generously if that's what our children want and need because it will pay dividends in the future. Some children may demand a slower approach, as for them touch and intimacy are things to be wary of. They may be distant or always on the move, not being able to stay still long enough to be cuddled. It is important I think to take opportunities where we can, even small ones, to soothe away the barriers. Interlinking little fingers, brushing hair, putting on socks, washing a face are all acts which help us to strengthen the bonds between each other.

As touch is so frightening for some children we may need to be very patient and imperceptibly persistent. One of my children was so active and fast that I literally had to grab her (in a nice way) and hug her and make a game of it. She would wriggle and slide out of a gentle hug so in the end I decided I had to take affirmative action. Don't get me wrong, I didn't jump out at her in the hallway and frighten her or anything like that. I would sit on the floor with my arms out-stretched and say, as if to myself 'My arms are aching, I need a big hug from my best girl, I wonder where she is.' Early on she would completely ignore me. I would have to say 'I think I need to find her' and crawl on my hands and knees and chase her around a bit saying, 'Mummy's coming to get a hug' and laughing (so it didn't sound sinister). I could gauge her reactions and always backed off if it was getting too much. Often I could only hug her for a few seconds but I would always say, 'Oh that is sooo lovely, I love hugging my best baby girl.' Slowly she was able to take longer hugs and eventually she would come and hug me voluntarily. Now we hug all the time (and I am sometimes the one running away).

I know that my methods were amateur and perhaps clumsy, but for me it is very important that a child can learn to experience the right kind of touch as positive and learn to ask for comfort. Again, I give the 'absolutely no research' warning, but the children I know who have had the greatest struggles have shunned physical comfort from a trusted adult, even when they are really suffering. It's tempting to follow their signals and leave our children alone, especially when we are new adoptive parents and feeling under-confident, but I really believe it is to their detriment if we do that. Sometimes I think they need us to come at them a bit.

It can be disheartening to share your life with a child who gives all the signals that they really don't want to be touched or to have any intimacy at all, or who go through the motions but without appearing to want or appreciate a hug or a kiss. It feels likes straight rejection, but again, we have to try really hard to hear the brittle voice, the voice that says, 'I'm scared of touch, touch hurts, I need time to learn how to trust.' Again it is time, patience, empathy, creativity and playfulness that will start to make a difference. And sometimes we could really do with professional help to coax our relationship with our child into life, to help create the spark that will ignite a life-long bond, because maybe we're doing our best and it just doesn't feel like enough. I didn't experience rejection for a long period of time, but even then at times I felt a bit hopeless and like giving up, so I get how hard it must be to want to share so much with a child who just can't go there with you yet. I get much comfort from the experts who say, 'It's never too late.' Even now, with our older children there are opportunities for touch, in fact now I really think about it, they come to me often (sometimes a little too often). I am frequently offered a hand to shake or a back to scratch or a foot to rub or a knee to tickle. I wonder if they are trying to tell me something.

When I look back at my own children's progression, and of course there is still plenty to come so I may yet be proved wrong, it has taken plenty of backward turns and loop-the-loops but has maintained a broadly linear progression. Frustrating as it is, periods of regression can be about the settling and hardening of knowledge and experience and the testing out of it too. In my experience, a period of regression is often followed by some big steps along Progress Road.

Moving forwards and getting older is a challenge for developmentally traumatised children for whom the world has already been experienced as a dangerous and frightening place. We must avoid trying to push them on before they are ready and becoming frustrated when behaviours we thought we had seen the back of return for a while, or behaviours we welcomed seem to disappear without trace. There may even be the appearance of regressive behaviours in areas which our children had previously never found difficult. This usually occurs right after we think to ourselves, 'Great, we got away with that one.' Resting on our laurels is a dangerous thing to do as an adoptive parent and not to be recommended.

I have a suspicion, a completely unproven suspicion, that regression and 'immaturity' sometimes get confused with learning difficulties. When given the right level of nurture and therapeutic parenting and teaching some children, including my own, can make remarkable progress, beyond what was ever expected of them. As with much of therapeutic parenting it is important not to become disheartened or resigned and to always maintain the long view.

'I didn't even touch it'

There are some aspects of adoptive parenting that one doesn't read about in books or learn about on courses which can leave one entirely unprepared. It is only once conversations with other adopters take place that certain light bulb moments occur. 'It's not just us' is the first thought. Others may then concur. Before long you can be sure that the particular behaviour you have been puzzling over is common in adoptive families. I can't tell you how many times I've been through this process. It would have been much easier if someone had warned me about all this from the start.

One of the reasons I wanted to write this unofficial guide was to shed some light on these common but unspoken about behaviours. When they are not aired the adoptive parent (and child) can wind up feeling crazed. When we can nod in agreement, feel a sense of community, we can get on and tackle the behaviour, free from guilt and accusations of hysteria and drama queenage.

A prime example is the damaging of things. Lots of things. All the time. Nice things. Things which were given by someone special. Things which rely on other things to work properly. Things which have an important use. Things which are nice to have around. Things which when damaged really, really bug you. Can you tell that this is something which particularly gets my goat?

The sheer amount of damaged and broken things in my life drives me to distraction. Only yesterday I did some baking with my child. Despite super-close supervision, after an hour my rubber bowl scraper had a bite out of it and my pallet knife blade was bent at 90 degrees to its handle. I would guess that over the years the breakages would amount to several metric tonnes. In my nightmares I am drowning in it: in tractor wheels, dolls' arms, snapped toothbrushes, bent cutlery, dehorned unicorns, a lidless musical box, a tailless mermaid, half a pair of sunglasses, pop-up books with no pop, a waterlogged Nintendo DS, scissored bathroom towels, split toothpaste tubes, dismembered dinosaurs, Playmobil tyres, Playmobil hair. I could go on, but I would risk working myself up into a lather and really the last thing a stressed adoptive parent (you) needs is to be bored to death by the travails of another stressed adoptive parent (me).

Lest it sound as though I am pouring blame upon my poor blameless children, I must point out that a number of the breakages are down to the adult members of the family providing toys and other items which our children were just not ready for, despite it being pretty flipping obvious. Whilst other children of similar ages were carefully and patiently playing 'Mousetrap' and 'Guess Who?' ours were pulling and tugging and biting anything they could get their hands on. I should have read my own section on Regression perhaps. But no, I so badly wanted our children to patiently play 'Mousetrap' and 'Guess Who?' that I made them available and might as well have said, 'Please break these as soon as possible.' I was setting them up to fail. So if you are struggling with the breakages thing, as I did, my first piece of advice is to take away the opportunities. We get cross when things get broken, and even though our children appear not to care, they do. They are just not going to show us they care. It's the shame thing again.

Anything valuable may just have to be put away for a few (a lot of) years. I could almost guarantee that if something was special to me, it would be targeted and an almighty row would ensue. Now I kind of conclude that if I've left something valuable out and it gets damaged then it's my fault. I have had to work particularly hard to 'rebrand' breakages as 'small stuff'. Not all breakages are small stuff of course. We can't ignore purposely broken windows and suchlike, but the majority of breakages are 'small stuff' and I am a lot more relaxed about them these days and barely notice most of it. As a result I am calmer and so are the children, which means that less stuff gets broken. It also means that if something important gets damaged then I don't need to make a scene to make a point – I've got headroom left because I haven't already shouted everyone into a ball of stress over something relatively minor. It's important to leave headroom.

One of the most powerful weapons to combat the breaking and damaging of things, in fact I would go so far as to state that it is the most powerful weapon of all, is, in my opinion, close supervision. I plant that seed now because you may feel like hitting me over the head with this book at the mere suggestion of it. You may be inwardly (or perhaps outwardly) screaming, 'You have no idea what my life is like, you think I've got the energy and time to do close supervision, you must be crazy.' Alright. Take a breath and forget about it for a while. It won't crop up again, other than in passing, until Chapter 11, Practical Techniques.

The lament of the laundry basket

Another under-written about and under-discussed issue which causes great distress and which parents and children need much more support with I think is what I shall delicately refer to as 'toilet troubles'.

Modern wonder-parenting leads us to believe that our children, healthily parented or otherwise, should be fully toilet trained by about three days old. There are these ancient cultures you see who manage it perfectly well and without any fuss and what's more there are small babies who can indicate with a special noise they need the toilet (although I'm told they're not great at washing their hands afterwards). How, then, does it make us feel when our child is still wearing night time pull-ups and bringing home carrier bags of wet clothes from school way after other children are taking part in competitive chess tournaments? Rubbish, that's what. Not only that, everyone including MPs and educational commentators feel free to pour bucket loads of smelly consternation into debates about how terrible it is that pre-school and even school-age children (gasp) are not fully toilet trained. It ranks alongside not being able to use a knife and fork properly and not being able to communicate clearly. Who are these savage children being raised by these barely civilised parents? I raise my hand. I could have ticked all of these boxes, and some, and the shame and guilt which I, let alone my children felt, did us no good at all. I applied pressure upon my children to be completely toilet trained before they were capable of it and for that, dear children, I am very sorry.

I may not be proud of how I sometimes managed the while toilet thing, but I forgive myself because of the enormous pressure I felt under to 'normalise' my children. I had no one else to consult with, no one who said to me, 'That's entirely normal, don't worry about it' and so I panicked a bit. Part of the problem is of course, as it so often is, that the received 'wisdom' is that children recover from trauma and neglect quickly and painlessly. Being left in a shitty, urine-soaked cot, hungry and scared for long periods of time, if it was inflicted on an adult would probably scar that adult for life. And adults have brains which work and thinking skills like reasoning and logic and coping mechanisms like hope. Small children don't have that. They have fear and self-loathing. And if you have a child with toilet problems and they, as far as you know, didn't suffer neglect, don't panic either. Scientists are only just starting to learn about the impact of the trauma of broken attachments on young children and babies, and the impact of pre-birth trauma like domestic violence. And as most of us know, fear can do funny things to the nether regions. So I would say, if you have an adopted child who has problems knowing when they need to go to the toilet, then don't waste too much time wondering why – deal with it therapeutically. It's not going to do any damage.

As well as fear and anxiety being barriers to toilet training, there is also the added issue of 'dissociation'. A child living an unbearable life is thought to cut themselves off from physical sensation as a means of survival. You may notice that your child will quite happily wear only a t-shirt in cold weather, or a thick jumper in the middle of the summer. Given that, perhaps it isn't actually that puzzling that they don't always pick up on the urge to go to the toilet. I wouldn't be surprised if in years to come (or it may have happened already), scientists discover in traumatised children some interruption in the messages sent from bladder and bowel to brain, at which point there will be many children turning to their parents saying, 'I told you I didn't know I needed to go to the toilet.'

There are times when the need to go is urgent and clear to everyone around. The wriggling, jiggling and trouser-tweaking is a give-away. Our children will still at this point look at you with unfettered disdain when you may dare to suggest that they might need to visit the small room. The self-esteem and trust in humanity to transition from what and who the child is engaged with, to a spell of time in the small room, is a bigger step than we might imagine. They may not yet have cemented the trust that what they leave behind will still be there when they get back. They may be struggling with planning ahead and consequential thinking. After all, we adults answer the call of nature because if we don't we will wet or shit ourselves and suffer the most terrible public humiliation imaginable as a consequence. We are able to project ahead, imagine the consequences and decide that we just don't want to go there. From that we form a habit, which we don't really have to think too much about. It seems like a simple process, but I'm not sure it is.

Enough of reasons. Reasons help with empathy and patience but there is always a need for practical suggestions.

After almost ten years of toilet troubles (less because initially the toilet problem wasn't a problem at all) and I now pretty much know what I'm doing, and bar the very occasional accident the problem has gone away. I know of course that in even writing this I am living dangerously. I still indulge in occasional rants about noxious smells in laundry baskets and suchlike, but that's me. I'm a 90 per cent of the time patient, 10 per cent of the time hot-headed with not much in between kinda woman. (My children may disagree with this ratio.)

I have learned that the key to cracking the toilet thing is fuss-free patience and acceptance. No amount of sighing or preaching is going to shift things. No number of sticker charts or reward chocolates will either. They may work temporarily, but we are looking for embedded and structural change here, not just doing something to win a prize. 'Don't worry about it, let's get you changed' and 'I know it's hard to understand when you need the toilet but we'll get there' and 'That must feel uncomfortable, let's get you dry and warm again' are the mantras that work. Change their clothes and comfort them with love in your heart and they will slowly learn that they are lovable and safe and that's gold dust.

We must also accept that we are likely to be doing a lot of laundry for a very long time. That's the way it is. There are ways of minimising the laundry burden, particularly bed wear and sheets. Plastic mattress protectors have saved my sanity (they work best with a towel and a fitted sheet over the top to prevent 'pooling' and 'running'). Pull-ups are helpful even when society is raising its eyebrows that your child still needs them. Ignore the pressure and do what's necessary to keep anxiety and shame to a minimum. Against all advice we woke our children every night and took them to the toilet. It worked for us. It drastically increased the chances of a dry night when nothing else worked and it cut down on my laundry load. After a year, or perhaps a little longer, they started waking up when they needed to go. We also installed a toilet upstairs to make getting up in the night a little less scary.

Eventually patience, habit and maturity prevail and the clouds will part and there will be mainly dry days and nights ahead.

Some of our children can take a bit of a backward step in the toilet training department when they start school. They might find it embarrassing to ask to use the toilet, or the toilet might feel a scary place to them. Teamed with these issues is the state of high anxiety that many of our children feel in the school environment. It is really important that the staff supporting our children take an empathetic and well-informed approach to toilet issues. It is worth taking time to explain to teaching staff that your child may experience difficulties and the reasons why. Keep spare clothes at school, just in case, and avoid the public 'wet trouser handover' at the end of the day (or you may as well put it in the school newsletter).

CHAPTER 6

THE HARD STUFF

The Hard Stuff is what keeps us awake at night, takes us to the very edge and tests us to the point where one day we find ourselves laid on the kitchen floor in our tracksuit bottoms sobbing into the biscuit crumbs and onion skins of life. If that's where you are now, and at the risk of making you feel temporarily worse, I reach out to you and offer you my shoulder to cry on. Living with the anger, aggression, violence, swearing, lying and stealing of a traumatised child is extremely and hideously difficult.

What makes it so much worse is that very few people really get what it is like parenting a full-on, High Definition, Dolby sound traumatised child. Some will seek to try to minimise our experience as though we have just got things out of perspective. They will say things like, 'All children do that' or 'It's a phase' or 'Have you tried using time-out?' If a neglectful past is mentioned then, well you know, the old chestnuts come out, 'They won't remember, it was too long ago' and 'Children are much more resilient than we realise'. It is utter hogwash as you know and I know, but it still delivers a low punch.

We are talking trauma here and smashed-up attachments, not a bit of misbehaving. They are very different things. Our children haven't read the usual parenting manuals and if they had would chew them up and spit them out, just for starters. That's my experience anyway.

The first message I want to pass on to you, as someone once gifted to me, is this: the causes of the trauma lie firmly in the past; you did not cause the trauma. It is obvious, and yet not obvious from the kitchen floor. The second message is this: every single adoptive parent has made mistakes, so forgive yourself. The third message is: tomorrow is a new day (it sounds trite but it's true). Now get yourself up off the floor, brush yourself down and go and put some proper trousers on.

Before you read on, if you really are in the depths of despair, if your nerves are shattered, if the thought of getting up to put a proper pair of trousers on makes you want to cry, then please turn to Chapter 10, Self-Care. Self-care is crucial for those of us parenting a traumatised child (or children) who is throwing the big stuff at us. Some of us are not very good at self-care. I would go so far as to say that it is a cornerstone of successful therapeutic parenting. Without it the building comes tumbling down and all is lost. So for goodness sake, take care of yourself.

'Red Brain'

I'm starting with ANGER because ANGER is the fastest route to hopelessness and fear I know. I am talking ANGER here, not anger. There is a BIG DIFFERENCE. If you live with an ANGRY child you will appreciate that ANGRY is not 'quite cross' and that MELTDOWN is not a bit of door slamming and name-calling. Lots of people don't get that difference. Lots of people supporting adoptive families don't get that difference.

You may be reading this as a friend or relative of an adopter or a professional supporting adopters or their children. Either way, it is crucial that you know what ANGER is in a traumatised child, even if you never witness it. These parents, your clients, your friends, your relatives did not get where they are because they are being a bit flaky, not setting enough boundaries, not being firm enough or rewarding enough. Trust me.

ANGER is a total and absolute loss of control. It is visceral, violent and animal. And it is very, very frightening. It makes you fear for your and your child's safety. Really, really fear for it. Like in a life and death way.

ANGER means the throwing of heavy objects, the heaving over of massive items of furniture, the smashing of lamps and pictures, the breaking of windows, the hitting of walls with little fists with bone-shattering force. It is running, jabbing and lashing like a tornado. It is the fight, flight, freeze response in full Technicolor. It is the sins of the past spilling out over the present. It is blood and bone, vomit, shit and piss.

After appalling natural disasters or crimes of terror victims wonder about the devastation in a state of blank, white shock. This is what it feels like once ANGER has blown over. You will recall only jumbled fragments of what happened. You find yourself unable to describe the events in a way which makes sense to anyone else. When the numbness has passed you might cry for a very long time, tears of utter and complete desperation.

I apologise if I stir up difficult feelings. I stir them up for myself too. My family endured a long period where ANGER gusted in perhaps twice a day, every day. It was so extreme I stopped feeling. I didn't cry anymore. I was haunted by a deep, dark, sickening fear. I thought my family was breaking apart and would never be stuck back together again.

I share this with you because we got help and that help and the therapeutic work it enabled us to carry out has got us to now. Now means a previously angry, confused, sad child is maturing into an emotionally intelligent, reflective, funny young person who can talk about feelings in a way that would outdo many adults I know. His healing is ongoing, but from a foundation of relative calm we make great progress.

From the start of our life together our son had anger about him. It was never far away. Although that has been difficult for him it has meant we have had no choice but to touch the trauma, look at it full in the face and journey through trauma and history together.

Our younger child has a deeper anger hidden and buried inside layers of controlled compliancy, humour, busyness and smiley happiness. I'm not suggesting that these traits are in any way fake, I'm just saying that they are an effective way of keeping everyone's eyes away from the pain, including her. The anger is starting to come, when it could no longer be contained, and now that her brother's anger no longer dominates family life.

Although both children's anger 'styles' are different, the therapeutic approaches we've taken are very similar and have worked and are working with both.

It is often difficult to identify what it is that lights anger's fuse. It might be hearing 'no', as in 'No not now, but you can have some cake after tea.' The resulting storm has far more attached to it than the cake. The cake is the match thrown into the box of fireworks. Sometimes being found out, being caught doing something off limits lights the fuse or the anger brews up during a difficult day at school and spills out at home. Sometimes you see ANGER gathering like a huge wave on the horizon and you watch it racing towards you with deep fear in your guts.

Each situation is different, but I have a few stakes in the ground which I share with our children when times are calm; I will not allow myself or anyone else in the house to be physically hurt, I will not allow the angry child to physically hurt themselves, I will not allow household items (other than minor things) to be smashed up. If any of these things become foggy or negotiable in any way then I think I would be in trouble. The last thing an angry, scared child needs is an adult who is floundering. They need us to be calm, close, strong and predictable in order that they feel safe. It is the time to get all the therapeutic stuff right. When I'm struggling I try to reimagine ANGER as the red-faced cry of a baby screaming for comfort.

You will know what inflames things in your home and what doesn't. I know that if I employ a calm 'therapy' voice it makes things much, much worse. It's the 'Calm down dear' approach, which I find infuriating too. I have to meet my children at least half way emotionally, which shows that I get where they are at.

It is tempting, during a storm, to leap, in panic, into traditional parent mode. 'Don't speak to me like that,' 'Don't you dare swear at me again,' 'If you throw that at me I'm taking your game away,' etc. Don't do it. DO NOT DO IT. You might as well run outside and scream into the wind for all the good it will do.

Once I have quickly secured everyone's safety as best I can, these are the sorts of things I've been coached to say and which have worked,

'I get that you are really angry right now.'

'I can understand why that made you angry.'

'I'm not going away. I'm staying with you to keep you safe.'

'It doesn't matter what you call me, I'm staying because I care about you.'

'I know that is your experience of mummies, that they leave you when you need them.'

Let's say they have run into a room and they are raging about. I will judge whether my presence is inflaming the situation and if I think it is then I say:

'I'm going to stand just outside the room and give you some time.'

'I will come back in one minute and check you are all right. You tell me if you need me before then.'

If heavy things are being thrown then I will take those things and say:

'I'm taking this because I don't want you to hurt yourself.'

In the past I have had to repeat this close checking in for an hour or two or more. During this time I will also be checking in with my other child who is likely to be over-hearing everything in a state of terror. It is important to show empathy for them too:

> 'I know it is scary when your brother is angry, but Mum is in control and looking after everyone.'

For a good long time all you may hear is 'F**K OFF' and its many variants. It is difficult to hear and I say that as someone who isn't that queasy about swearing, but it is important not to take it personally. Instead of seeing a raging, swearing, hate-fuelled child, try instead to see a child in pain and grief and terror because that's really truly where they are. They are so scared, ashamed and uncomprehending they can't express themselves any other way, that is, until they've been given the tools to do so.

In our family an episode like this will often end up being all about life story work: the sharp end of life story work.

> 'I wonder if all that rage and hurt inside you is about something much bigger than there not being any biscuits left.'

> 'I wonder if it reminded you of feeling hungry.'

> 'I think you have a right to feel angry about what happened to you. I do too.'

> 'I feel angry and sad about it as well. It was wrong.'

And like the great Dr Dan Hughes (whom I have learnt much of this from) says, it's acceptable, if not necessary, for us to show our child our sadness. I have expressed these feelings before with tears in my eyes and it has given my child permission to feel sad for themselves.

'I wish I could have been there to protect you and take care of you' is where we often end up.

All of these phrases have helped to crank open the heavy door. What usually comes is a great resolution, when I can cradle my sad, hurting child and tell them I love them so very much.

This kind of scenario has taken place in our family many times but something significant usually shifts as a result. The next time a little more is shared and expressed and resolved. There is a real sense that important work is taking place.

Some of our children have had to put up strong barriers in order to keep themselves protected, and will test us to find out whether it is safe to let them down. Some of the anger may be about whether we are going to be strong enough to last the course with them, show ourselves to be strong enough to share the pain with, trustworthy enough to be allowed to know the truth. It is a test we must pass if our children are going to stand any chance of learning that their pasts were not their fault. My older child put great effort into bringing about what he saw on some level as inevitable: going back into care (he had watched this play out in an adoptive family we are friends with). Once he realised, with some help from a therapeutic social worker, that Mum and Dad were going to be with him for the long run, he kind of gave up the fight and relaxed into family life. He didn't really know he was doing this on a conscious level, but in voicing it to him in an 'I wonder' way and reiterating our determination, strength and love, something fell into place. That was almost two years ago now and there has barely been any raging since then. What rage there has been is about the outside world: friendships and school mainly.

Something I have learned directly from our son is the importance of voicing all the good therapeutic stuff, even if it appears not to be registering. 'I remember every single thing you say to me when I'm angry and after I'm angry,' he said recently.

I never give a consequence as a result of ANGER (there, I said it). I don't want to punish my child for being scared and sharing something difficult with me. At most I would encourage them to clear up any resulting mess with me and use the opportunity to talk a bit more about what happened. One time my child threw everything he could find which connected him to me down the stairs. I was able to say, 'You were CROSS with me, I wonder if you thought I was saying "no" to hurt you' and it opened up a whole new seam entitled, 'Why mothers are not to be trusted,' which we investigated together.

In my experience, once the storm has passed (and we have reached the shocked, zombified stage), our children will be mortified that they behaved in this way. It is important to stay close to them, show them you love them, but it's also appropriate I think to explain how you feel, bearing in mind that we should keep shame to a minimum. Finally, once your partner comes home, or your friend comes over, or your child is in bed, do what you need to do to get the feelings out. Cry. Run. Listen to loud music. Drink wine. Eat chocolate. Rage a bit. Write it down. Wrap yourself inside a duvet. This bit is very important.

If you are the partner of someone who has just endured a monumental storm whilst you've been out, try your very best not to judge. Listen and empathise. Listen and empathise. And take over the entire bedtime routine and any other outstanding domestic duties. And if your child greets you all smiles and loveliness, try not to be fooled: that's what they do. It's a survival mechanism.

ANGRY children can be extremely provocative. Not even 'can be', 'are'. My children have needed to take me right to the edge to find out what I'm made of. Will I hit them, scream at them or act in any way like an abusive parent? They need to know. 'Bring it on' they say. I admit here that I have lost my temper lots of times. I was tempted to use the word 'several' instead of lots to describe how often I've 'gone off on one', but in the interests of honesty I must be truthful. I mentioned earlier that I am someone who's temper stays out of sight for 90 per cent of the time and the other 10 per cent of the time it leaps out of my mouth like a flamethrower. My anger shocks and frightens me (much like theirs does them). Nowadays we have much less anger in our house, but when I feel mine rising I try to press the 'pause' button and say, 'I am feeling really angry and so I'm going to walk away for a few minutes and calm down.' This is anger management in action. If I go wrong and I still do, I always apologise afterwards:

> 'I'm really sorry I shouted. I should not have reacted like that.'

As our children have got older and more adept at the language of emotion, I've shared more with them about how their insults affect me. They need to learn that they can't call me a 'fat b***h' and expect me to shrug it off. After all, it doesn't happen like that outside our front door.

After a day of ANGER a good bedtime is particularly important. We will be feeling injured and exhausted and want to remove ourselves physically and emotionally. No matter how the ANGER played itself out, our child will lie in the darkness and reflect on what monsters they are. After ANGER has called I always try my best to muster up the energy and positivity to give them a bedtime kiss and say something like:

> 'I know today was hard and you were angry and I was angry, but I love you no matter what and tomorrow is a new day.'

Then you can go back to raging, or crying, or sitting zombie-like gazing at the ceiling.

With older children who are starting to develop more self-control and reflective skills it might be possible to take a more robust approach. I can with my eldest child, but I still need to judge the situation carefully. If he has really over-stepped the mark then I might try:

> 'I can't be with you right now because what you said really offended me.'

If Mr D. is at home then we perform a bit of a double-act.

'You hurt Mum's feelings so you need to give her some time on her own,' he will say.

I wouldn't try this with a younger child who can't cope with the separation and I wouldn't pull it out of the hat too often, but in our family it has shifted things in the right direction. It is the start of encouraging our children to reflect on how their actions impact upon others.

Once the storm has passed it is tempting, once the sabre-toothed tiger is sleeping, to try to forget all about it for fear of poking it back to life. This is certainly my 'go to' response, particularly when I've been badly bruised and feel like booking into a bed and breakfast far, far away. I have been taught that this 'Let's move on' response is really 'Let's brush the sabre-toothed tiger under the carpet' where it is obvious to everyone as they step around it, pretending not to have noticed it. Our children will of course be very aware of the tiger under the carpet. They will be aware of very little else as the shame associated with the episode engulfs them. They may well be very good at pretending to have moved on from the episode. You may find yourself digging your nails into the palm of your hand at the sound of them laughing and making light. They need 'situation normal' to return as soon as possible. 'Situation normal' means pain can be ignored.

This is what I've been taught to do after ANGER has passed and it has proved to be effective. Once calm has been restored we must return to the events with the child and reflect in a storytelling way. Something like this:

> 'You were getting ready to go out really well yesterday and then Dad couldn't help you with your shoes at the moment you needed him to and goodness you got really angry.'

This is not delivered in a telling-off or a bland voice, but a lightly animated, non-confrontational voice.

> 'And I know that you said and did some things that you didn't mean to [you may need to name them] and I want you to know that I still love you.'

Then a hug if they can manage it and then:

> 'I'm looking forward to going out with you today, we're going to have a great time.'

In thera-speak, this is creating a narrative of the event using the past, the present and the future which the child can use to try to make sense of what happened. As our children have got older I have added a little extra along the lines of:

> 'Let's have a think about how we could have handled it better' particularly if there was a tipping point (a point at which it all went wrong).

We will both reflect on how we could have done better. I then return to the scenario the next time a similar situation presents itself:

> 'At this point you could either brush your hair and get in the car and go out with Dad and have a good time, or what might happen?'

If this goes to plan the response might be:

> 'Dad will go without me and I will get very angry.'

This technique can interrupt the descent into ANGER and teaches the thinking out of consequences. Our children have needed a lot of support with this and yours may do too. If the right choice is made, even with bad grace, then top off with a quick and smart teaspoon of praise:

> 'Well done for making the right choice' is enough.

If the wrong choice is made then top off with a dessert spoon of empathy:

> 'I know it's hard for you to make good choices sometimes. I'm going to continue to help you with that.'

If all this sounds like highly-complicated brain gymnastics, it is. With practice it gets easier and then becomes second nature and really quite obvious. You may find yourself thinking, 'Why can't we all just get ready and go out and have a lovely day without all these shenanigans?' You and me both. The way I see it, though, is that we can either force them to make a good choice by threatening them with something (which doesn't work chez Donovan), or we can teach them the life-long thinking skills they need to make good choices themselves.

When unwise choices are being made frequently or at a time of day when I don't have the time or energy for the brain gymnastics I will use a more 'traditional' method: 'just do it' or similar. Sometimes it works. Sometimes it doesn't. That's real life for you.

Long after ANGER has passed over I sometimes like to carry out a kind of 'lessons learned' exercise: an 'If it happens again what can we do better?' I do it in an inquisitive and enquiring way because what do I know about how it feels to be in the grip of terrifying, disabling anger? Actually very little. Once I asked my son how it feels and he came out with the term 'Red Brain'. He described being completely out of control and frightened and unable to make choices. He said that it is as though his brain has been taken over and gripped by something terrifying and outside of himself. At the same time he is frightened that he is going to hurt someone dear to him and scared that he doesn't have the control to prevent himself from doing so. We've worked out lots of systems together.

At it's peak, our son's ANGER was like nothing I have ever witnessed before in my life. Gradually, though, the anger played out over a shorter and shorter time and became less physical. In its latter stages I could rescue my son from it before it took hold:

> 'Your sister was in the wrong then. I completely understand why that angered you. Let's walk the anger off outside.'

Or something similar.

Then he became able to pull himself back from Red Brain without any help. These days he is mostly calm and uses many of the coping strategies we have learnt together.

I will leave you at the end of this roller coaster section with some extracts from a piece which our son wrote for my blog. It is addressed first to a younger child who was struggling with the same anger issues that he was:

> *I have experienced the anger you have, I know it's horrible. We named the anger 'Red Brain.' Yeah it's a horrible thing to grow up with but it gets better honestly ☺ It won't come out as*

much as you get older. It is NOT your fault so don't blame it on yourself!!!!

When you feel Red Brain coming you should just tell your mum or dad and then remove yourself from the situation you're getting angry in. When you do have the 'Red Brain', you say all these words to your mum or dad, but they will know it's not your fault they might feel a bit hurt or sad (they will recover in a few days).

Note: One of the standards I set myself, throughout all my work, is honesty. Honesty and adoption and trauma are not always easy bedfellows, but dishonesty does nothing for children and families living through extreme times. I read back this section and had to admit to myself that I'd skipped, rather deftly I thought at the time I wrote it, one very important piece of information. I skipped over it because I wasn't feeling brave enough to put it in, not because I don't stand by it and because I worry that my words will get bent out of shape by those who really don't get what it's like living with a severely dysregulated and red hot angry child. If you are living with such a child then I'll bet you noticed. It comes right where I wrote, 'I will not allow myself or anyone in the house to be physically hurt.' 'How does she do that?' you may have thought, or words to that effect. The answer is I used something I was taught by a social worker called 'safe hold'. You need to be taught safe hold by someone who knows what they're talking about. It's not something I can describe here but basically, so you get that I'm not some kind of child abuser, it is a big, firm hug accompanied by confidently and clearly spoken reassurances like, 'I'm here to keep you safe,' 'I know you're scared,' 'I'm not going to let you hurt yourself.' The experts call it 'co-regulation'.

Safe hold was nothing short of a game changer for our family. Within a couple of weeks of being taught how to do it and having used it only a handful of times, the anger died down and our child began to learn how to regulate himself. Then the anger virtually disappeared which bought us time to do all the good therapeutic work which is impossible when heavy objects are being thrown at your head and you are so angry, hurt and desperate that you can barely function. It was during this time of peace that we put our family back together and made unexpected and glorious progress.

'What's yours is mine'

There are certain behaviours that get to us, panic us and send us running back into the welcoming arms of traditional parenting. For me, that's stealing. I hesitate to call it 'stealing' because the word makes what might actually be hoarding, gathering and borrowing sound kind of serious and criminal. If there's one thing we need to avoid it is making our children feel like criminals.

Seen in the context of their backgrounds of neglect and loss, taking things is understandable, especially when paired with a lack of consequential thinking and impulsivity.

'Taking things' covers a whole range of behaviours. It means your child takes something of yours which they covet, or they take money from you, or they take something which they know will have an impact on you. I'm not going to include food here, as to me it's a different tin of biscuits altogether.

For a long while items like deodorant, hair gel and old mobile phones went missing and subsequently turned up in school bags. They were being taken to show off to and impress others. Mr D. and I used to get really exercised about this kind of taking, but looking back now, it was small stuff. We shouldn't have made a big deal about it and instead just empathised with the desire to fit in and impress others.

The big stuff for me is taking money and I do call that stealing. It has been an issue which has proven difficult (but not impossible) to unstick. It started when both children started to get pocket money and one would secretly take money from the other. It really got me cross, 'How could you take money from your sister/brother?' I would rant uselessly to the soundtrack of multiple denials and accusations.

On advice from our social worker I bought both our children locking money boxes which worked until the keys were taken and money disappeared again. We now hide the keys and keep a paper record of weekly pocket money and any extra earned through doing chores. It is a pain in the neck having to run everything like a PTA treasurer, but it avoids lots of failure and anguish.

When larger amounts of money started being taken from my purse or from my husband's wallet or pockets, things got harder. I felt (and still do from time to time) a bitterness that I couldn't keep my money safe in my own home. It was like I had been invaded and in sneaky and crafty ways. On occasion I thought back and realised I had been manipulated in order that a child could gain access to my bag. After the deed had been done, that same child would then be all over me, falling over themselves to be lovely and helpful and kind.

'Can I make you a cup of tea Mummy dearest?' and that kind of thing.

I would feel like a fool and started to doubt all positive advances, unsure whether they were genuine or part of a scam. It impacted upon my sense of myself and my feelings of safety in a deeper and more unsettling way than the anger and aggression ever did. I became hyper-alert to where everyone was in the house at any one time, where my bag was, where money was hidden and what it was being spent on. It drove me a little bit bonkers. To be honest, when we are encountering another spell of taking money, it still does. Perhaps I should lighten up a bit but actually, taking money from someone else has to be one of those values that we mark with a stake in the ground. It is wrong. No excuses. However, that doesn't mean that we abandon our therapeutic methods. In fact, they are more important then ever when we are faced with unacceptable behaviours like these.

The dilemma is how do we tackle stealing without increasing feelings of shame and without making the problem worse?

I have had a lot of help with this, and so I need to give credit to our social workers for the wise advice I have been given, which I pass on here.

Incidents of stealing often increase during times of stress. It can be any of the usual suspects: starting a new school, going on holiday, going to a big social event, going out with friends. In our family it is heightened around school fair time and school disco time when a head of steam builds up around the prospect of being able to buy drinks, sweets and tat with a free rein. They just can't cope with it. It blows every fuse in the circuit. The pocket money given to them is not enough. They must buy and consume as much as possible. And with less supervision than normal a sort of wildness overtakes them.

We have employed a number of strategies. First is avoidance. It is fine and well insisting that our children, because they are x years old, should be able to cope with a school fair or whatever it is, but if they can't, then they can't. No amount of wishing or lecturing is going to change that. We are sometimes advised to 'think toddler' when it comes to our children, and I think this is a good situation in which to do that. Would we allow a toddler to walk on their own around a school fair with a couple of pounds in their sticky hands? No. But unless I lassoed my children to me there is no way I would be able to make them stay by my side in such situations. So if I suspect they are going to fail by taking money and then eating their own bodyweight in honeycomb, then we don't go to the fair. I would never tell them why we are not going to the fair because that would be far too shaming (so none of that 'We aren't going because last year you took money from me and spent it on two kilos of peanut brittle'). We have to be more clever than that. This is what I do,

> 'I know this is going to be really disappointing because you've been looking forward to the school fair so much, but we won't be able to go this year.'

(Lots of moaning and wailing.)

> 'We're going to be doing something much, much more fun which we arranged to do ages ago.'

I'll leave you to think up the fun thing which is going to compete with the school fair. It had better be good though.

The second strategy is to hide all money away. In our house we really have to hide it away, in really bizarre places, because our children are brilliant at finding it (if 'brilliant' is the right word). Our oldest child talks about the absolute compulsion he has felt in the past to locate and take the cash. He says that the thinking part of his brain doesn't get a look in. The way I see it, it is compassionate to take away opportunities for our children to steal when they feel this way.

Third, we have opened up a dialogue with our children, as I allude to above, about how they feel when they are in the grip of needing to take money. By approaching a hot subject in a cool and inquisitive way we have learnt a lot about the nature of the behaviour and how it can be prevented from taking place. 'Help me to understand' is always a good starter.

Last, are consequences. I'll come out here, contrary to some advice, and declare that we give consequences for taking money, not a few coppers here and there, but proper amounts. The only consequence we give is doing chores, alongside us, to earn the money back, if the money has been spent. If the money hasn't been spent then it is returned and a lesser chore is carried out, alongside us, in order to make up for what has been done. What I've learnt not to do is to take away money as a repayment which the child already owns, or has earned. In our family that is a direct route to shame and anger. It is important to ensure that the consequence is secondary to the discussion which needs to take place about the behaviour. Something like this:

> 'I get that you wanted to buy sweets on your way to school, because you love sweets and I do too, but it isn't acceptable to take money.'

This needs to be done in a calm but meaningful tone of voice. If the behaviour has persisted it might be worth trying the narrative technique which I covered earlier in this chapter. Something like:

> 'You've been doing well lately in not taking money from Dad, but today you slipped up because you saw something you wanted to buy. We're going to make up for it by doing something nice for Dad.'

The 'doing something nice for Dad' is not only a recompense; it gives close-supervision time which can reap extra benefits. When both of you are engaged in an activity and chatting at the same time, things might be shared that wouldn't otherwise be if the child felt more 'under the spotlight'. It's a bit like the conversations we have in cars as we're negotiating that busy motorway interchange in the dark. You know the ones. And of course the strong message being given by us to our child is that despite their behaviour, we are choosing to spend time with them. It might sound counter-intuitive, but once you get into the swing of therapeutic parenting it really isn't. It is demonstrating that we might not be that impressed by what they've done, but we still love them and delight in them. If our children were ever going to benefit from being ignored and given 'time-out', they would already be the best-behaved kids in the village.

Just sometimes it is worth trying something off-the-wall in response to a big behaviour like stealing, something so bizarre that it shakes the raisins to the top of the muesli packet, something that stops the fight, flight, freeze response in its tracks. It's risky but sometimes it works a treat.

Some years ago a ten pound note disappeared from my purse. It was ten minutes before we were due to leave for school. I found it in a school bag. I had the immediate need to shout and scream but I held myself back. As there was lots going on at the time an immediate consequence would have just got lost in the noise. I sensed that I needed to make an impact in a different way. I replaced the ten pound note with a short letter which said something like:

> 'I don't think you meant to take the money so I've taken it back and we'll talk about it later, love Mum xx.'

When I picked him up after school he still, despite my note, looked terrified.

> 'We're going into town to buy a takeaway for tea. What would you like?'

He looked at me as though I had gone crazy. It was not what he had been expecting and what he was primed for. There was nothing for him to fight against, argue with, get angry about.

> 'But I took money from you and now you're doing something nice for me.'

> 'Yep.'

On the way to the takeaway we talked a bit about why he had wanted to take the money and what the frenzy felt like. I knew he was sorry. He has a strong sense of right and wrong. It felt like another big step along Progress Road.

I would love to report that he never took money again, but I can't. It has happened several times and I haven't always managed to respond in such a calm way. The last time it happened was the day before we were due to have three tonnes of gravel delivered which needed to be wheelbarrowed some distance. We all pitched in and it was fun as well as hard work. At the end of the day he said:

'I am never, ever taking money again. Sorry.'

Since then he has felt able to warn me when he feels tempted.

'You need to hide your bag, I feel like I might take something.'

I will always reply, 'Thanks for telling me,' and then we talk a bit about what has brought on that feeling.

I don't know whether or not that's the end of it, but the likelihood is less and the foundations on which to deal with it are stronger.

When I have reacted to stealing badly, when I've fallen back into the traditional methods, it never ends well. No one confesses no matter how much heat I apply, there will be accusations and cross-accusations, mud-flinging and aggressive counter-measures. I have often ended up feeling like the perpetrator and they will paint themselves as the victims. It is psychological warfare on a grand scale, so grand that I am left doubting everything I ever knew to be true about the event. It is tempting to walk into the battlefield. We have right on our side. We must emerge victorious and strong. But there are no good guys and bad guys in this story. For me the most important part is not reacting as soon as I discover the missing money; if I do, I react badly. I have to walk away, divert my anger and plan. Often Mr D. has to talk me down.

The issue of stealing is made a whole lot more complicated when siblings are involved. There is less certainty and the strong possibility that someone has been framed. I'm going to talk more about the detective work required where there are siblings in Chapter 7, Brothers and Sisters, but for now I'll just say that not every incident can be solved, unless that is you have CCTV, which, although tempting, is taking things a little too far.

Pants on fire

In our house lying comes in waves. Some of these waves have been so massive they have broken above our heads and threatened to wash us all away. Lying doesn't sound that serious an issue, neither does fibbing or telling stories, but some traumatised children, at times of stress, seem to be driven to lie about almost everything, almost all of the time. The lies can drive a great wedge between you all as doubt and lack of certainty become the flavour of the day. Trust is one of the foundation stones of healthy relationships, and when it's absent, it doesn't feel as though there is much to fall back on.

Lying can be over something important, like whether a misdemeanour has taken place, or something trivial, like cleaning teeth.

'Have you cleaned your teeth?' I might ask casually.

'Yes,' will come the reply.

I might discover that the toothbrush is dry.

We may then hold a debate over whether the toothbrush, which is undeniably dry, has been used to clean teeth with. We will even debate the dryness or otherwise of the toothbrush, how long a toothbrush takes to dry (a debate I will not win despite having the laws of logic and physics on my side).

The only response, apart from a little light curiosity, is close supervision, sometimes carried out through gritted teeth.

Lying can be about creating a better world, one where exciting things happen, races are won, top marks are gained. I was once told that a particular award was going to be given at a huge assembly to which a hall full of parents had been invited. I had been entirely hooked in by the reporting of the award. As I watched the little lie unravel on the stage I felt sick. I felt sick because a little part of me wanted it to be true, just as a big part of him wanted it to be true too. I had to get a grip and remind myself that he had imagined a better life for himself. We met in the playground afterwards. He sheepishly started to try to explain that he'd been assured by 'miss' that he would get the award.

'I can understand why you wanted it so badly, but it makes no difference to me, you're doing really well.'

I must admit that I drove home in a little cloud of grief, not for me, but for him and what should have been but isn't, just yet.

There are times when something major has taken place and that something major can't be ignored. It could be that a significant amount of money has been taken, or someone has cut a hole in your new sofa, or hidden something valuable and electrical in the washing basket. You will no doubt have your own unique major things. When confronted over such an occurrence, in my experience the traumatised child's first reaction will be to lie. It's the way they operate. It is self-protection and the lie can trip off the tongue as easily as honey off a spoon. Most of us have been brought up to take quite strongly against lying. It is the sure sign of the criminal mind, especially when the lies are so well delivered, and they are. I have often marvelled at how skillfully a child can construct an alternative reality when during normal conversation they are usually quite tongue-tied and limited in vocabulary. It is as though a normally unaccessed part of the brain becomes available to them. I've noticed the same when they really, really want to argue with you. The Oxford Union Debating Society has nothing in comparison.

Those parenting one adopted child will know the culprit straight away and can bypass the painful part of the process: trying to work out 'who done it'. In these more straightforward situations it is best I think to reach for the Dan Hughes box of tricks which contains playfulness, love, acceptance, curiosity and empathy (PLACE). For me empathy is the bedrock. If we can't at least understand why our children don't want to be found out, why they feel such shame at being caught doing some something 'bad' and why they need to protect themselves at all costs, then the other tools don't work so well. In the face of solid denials I go to 'I wonder', which is my phrase of first resort.

'I wonder why someone would cut a hole in the sofa,' I might ask curiously whilst simultaneously digging my finger nails into my palms and scrunching up my toes.

I also express how I'm feeling about it:

'It has made me feel angry and sad. I really like that sofa and it cost a lot of money.'

Now this bit is not in the books and I'm not recommending it, but sometimes I have said:

'Bloody hell, I can't believe that someone has done that. I need to go upstairs and calm down'

and worse.

What the books don't always appreciate is that the hole in the sofa may come right after £30 has been nicked from your purse, your birthday chocolates have been secretly eaten and the school have rung about a 'regrettable incident'. Life is not always (almost never) neat. If I am hopping mad, then I have no option but to show it; it spills out. I will have to leave the room and literally pace in a frantic and consumed way. I may sometimes throw things. I may say, loud enough so they can hear:

'Bloody hell, I'm angry!'

But despite being fuming angry, I have never hurt anyone, and that's the lesson. Mum is angry but predictable. My anger sessions are even a source of some amusement now and I am able to reflect on my anger style with them.

'Mum you stay really, really calm and then you really go off,' they can say.

They even compare other people's anger to mine.

'Mrs So-and-So at school, wow when she gets angry she is much more scary then you are,' they say. (And I think to myself, blimey, Mrs So-and-So sounds like a right witch.)

Anyway, I digress.

The lying can be more exasperating than the thing that the lie is trying to cover up. It feels like an insult, to have your things wrecked and then to be lied at. We want to say things like, 'Why can't you just tell the truth?' even though we know the answer ('Because you will get angry and my life will be in danger').

At times the best that can be achieved is, 'I get why you are finding it hard to tell me about that.' It may not be satisfying, but on some level it goes in. I am certain of that.

We may need to keep our child extra-safe for a while to prevent them from failing again and by stepping up the supervision. For example, we may need to remove the tiny, but sharp penknife from the bathroom, even thought we've kept it there for 25 years and it's really useful. (I'm still not over the sofa-slashing incident. Can you tell?)

We may want to introduce the idea of a shared chore to make up for the incident, but if our child is still maintaining that they had nothing to do with it, despite all evidence to the contrary, then this might be tricky. In this situation they may truly believe that they didn't do it.

As our children have got older, the softly softly, curious approach has resulted in some spontaneous confessions. These are quite miraculous when they appear and I always try to accept them with grace. They are the green shoots of guilt which haven't been stamped on by shame.

The type of lying that gets right under my skin and gets my goat is the fantastical, dramatic variety. 'Our bus came off the road today and turned over twice and then the air ambulance had to come and take the driver away' might be me exaggerating but it's not that far from the sort of thing I used to hear every day. 'So and so called me a big fat loser retard today and then punched me in the head and threw my bag in the mud.' 'My friend has cancer and his dad is a fast jet pilot and crashed into the sea.' In the past I have fallen hook, line and sinker for some of these fictions and have ended up looking like an idiot as a result. Many involve school and how hideously a teacher has behaved. The accounts are convincing and heart-felt and full of emotion. During times of higher then average stress almost everything that is said is either untrue or exaggerated. Those who have not experienced this may not appreciate how debilitating it is to live with. I have used a mixture of approaches, from the anti-therapeutic, 'Really? Do you think I'm some kind of fool?' to the more touchy-feely, 'Goodness, that sounds terrible, are you alright, it must have been scary?' Challenging the story will almost always end up in great offence being taken. When it's appropriate and practical (or I'm just plain fed up of the sanity-crushing lies) I have sometimes proven the story wrong, by presenting the undeniable facts. I try my hardest not to do this in a 'gotcha'-type way but to be gentle and curious. After all, to them, a dramatic story is life-affirming and gets them noticed and might be closer to the way in which they perceive the world than we might think. I'm not sure that any methods really make a great difference to this kind of storytelling, other than increased feelings of safety and security and increased self-esteem. It's all the other good work we do that ends up making a difference.

I must say a few words here about parenting adopted siblings in relation to lying. I wrote in my first book *No Matter What* about how siblings fight for every scrap of love, as though it is limited and as though it is a matter of life and death. This is their experience of love and nurture, and in my experience is amongst the most hard-wired survival mechanisms they have. It is one of the reasons why parenting adopted siblings is so very complex.

For a child whose existence feels threatened by a brother or sister, no matter how much they love that brother or sister, what better way to see them in the dog house than to set them up and then take pleasure in watching them getting into trouble. I have had my brain tied up in knots over something which has been reported by one that the other has allegedly done. The conclusion I have come to is never to take a tale at face value. There is no such thing as the innocent tale. The teller will get most hot under the collar that you are refusing to act upon the intelligence they have so generously provided you with, they will claim that you never believe them, that you favour their sibling, but it is a dangerous place to go. I have been there many times. It is best to acknowledge why they may need to get their sibling into trouble and to empathise with it. I've also learnt not to discipline one child in front of the other but to say, 'I will deal with it later. I'm in charge here.'

Verbal abuse or 'I f*****g hate you b***h'

That's a strongly worded title. Does it have a place in a book like this? It doesn't appear in other books about parenting. Not one I've ever read. And that's the reason it's here. I wish I could go further and write the words in their surround-sound entirety, but I'm guessing the book would then have to have a health-warning on the front and there would be much tutting.

Like it or not, the reality for many adoptive parents living with traumatised children is that this kind of insult and worse gets launched at them during times of stress and anger. I have now, I think, heard them all, in every colourful and creative combination. Lucky me.

I'm not saying that all traumatised children lob around language like this, or that they do so very often. You may never hear it. Or you may hear it from time to time with a venom that takes your breath away.

It is of course the product of a traumatised brain which has gone into panic. It is the fight of the fight, flight, freeze response. It may also be something to do with emotional pain relief.

I am no stranger to the occasional swear word myself. I might even say that I enjoy a bit of swearing. I swear in the car, I swear at the television, I swear about things that have really pissed me off. Although I try hard not to, I swear in front of our children sometimes. And that's naughty, I know. But even with a high tolerance to swearing, the abusive swear (and more so the chilling cold, cruel insult) really gets me straight into fight, flight or freeze. Sometimes the abuse might be fired off in the middle of anger and destruction and so it kind of gets lost amongst the flying shoes. But it always comes back to haunt me later when I'm sat amongst the debris of the day, wondering what on earth has just happened. It might be swearing or it might be, 'You're not my real mum,' 'You're no one and everyone wants you gone,' or 'You should just go and kill yourself.' Everyone has their own personal tender points I guess.

Some years ago when we were working with a therapeutic social worker he addressed the subject of abusive language during one of our sessions. His method was to take some of the sting out of the words.

'So you called your dad a 'w****r' and a 'c**t'? They are STRONG words. You must have been VERY VERY angry.'

He repeated the words over and over until they didn't seem so red hot, whilst our child writhed on the floor (and I sat wondering if I was having an out-of-body experience). Gradually the shame got diluted and we were able to talk about the anger itself and where it had come from. There was still a voiced unacceptance of the behaviour though.

'It isn't right to call your dad those things,' he said.

We have always had an 'open door' policy when it comes to swearing. After all, children hear words at school and don't always know what they mean. I would much rather they asked me what they mean rather than some other child. This policy has resulted in some bizarre and sometimes toe-curling conversations such as, whilst reading *Charlie and the Chocolate Factory*, age ten:

'That reminds me I have a word to ask you about later.'

We were reading a section about Willy Wonka. I'll leave you to work out where that conversation went. Clue: we're talking Wonka here, not Willy.

We grade each word according to its offensiveness. Willy Wonka would be a 9 out of 10, whilst the 'c' word would score a full 10. 'Arse' would be a 4, although you wouldn't use it in front of grandparents. 'Shit' scores a 6 and 'crap' scores a 5 (yes, even though Homer Simpson uses it). This system has helped our children to understand rude words and naughty words and I think that's important. At least, then, when you get a 10 out of 10 fired at you there is no doubt in anyone's mind that it is completely unacceptable.

Lots of things get said when anger is underway that shouldn't be acted upon, but top-rate verbal abuse isn't one of them in my book. It's another stake in the ground.

'We don't speak to each other like that in our house.'

After the 'c**t' and 'w****r' episode Mr D. had a servant for the day who brought him iced drinks and sandwiches and switched over to *Football Focus* for him and helped him clear out the garage.

Our therapeutic social worker reminded me of the importance of the ongoing work we need to do to keep shame levels to a minimum. He recommended checking in with phrases like:

'Have you felt like calling me a 'c**t' lately? No? Well that's progress.'

I must remember to keep doing this. It's easy to want to forget it ever happened.

It has always interested me that when we are out as a family and we hear a person openly swearing in the street, particularly if we hear a mother using a swear word at her child, our children are morally outraged and quite scared by it. Mr D. once took our eldest child to a Premiership football match. All our child could report back from the whole experience was that there was a man stood behind them who swore really badly and frequently. I think that on some level our children remember being in households where verbal abuse signalled a genuine, physical threat to their wellbeing. If this is the case then, as non-abusive parents, we need to de-couple swearing from lack of safety by discussing swear words and their relative power and purpose. However, it is perfectly reasonable for our children (as we are) to be wary of adults swearing in the street and to feel and express disgust at parents verbally abusing children in public. In our family there's always a need to talk about such incidents afterwards: why it is unacceptable and why children and adults deserve to be treated with respect.

Impression of a doormat

A step down from verbal abuse, yet still very much hard stuff, is constant, mind-numbing, paralysing rudeness. I don't just mean the occasional sigh or eye-roll; I mean when every exchange is barbed by what feels like malice, but isn't. It becomes part of the wallpaper of life, habitual, and before we know it we are one of those parents we didn't want to be, taking rudeness like some kind of pathetic victim. The trouble with rudeness is it can cause us to respond in less than therapeutic ways (or is that just me?). The less than therapeutic ways don't work and before we know it we are ground down and abusiveness has become just the way we all speak to each other. When we get cross and lecture, the perpetrator may just laugh in our faces or make silly noises and mock our intentions to regain control.

I don't like to see parenting as a battle for control, but in this situation I think it is. If adoptive parents show any kind of prolonged weakness or flakiness, then the message it sends our children is that we are not going to be strong enough to last the course with them. Subconsciously they seem to have a need to lead us to the edge of a very high cliff and make us beg to be allowed to jump off. They may, at the 11th hour, be terribly nice because they want a lift somewhere, then once the taxi run has been completed, you'll be back on the edge of the cliff, begging for the end to come. This sounds dramatic, I know, and if you haven't experienced it yourself you may find me cruel in my interpretation of what's going on here. Some readers, I am certain, will know exactly what I'm talking about.

If you find yourself deciding not to dish out a consequence or a warning because you are fearful of how your child might react, then you are on dangerous ground. I'm not meaning to lecture, because I've been there myself. Living in fear of a child is not what being a good parent is. We've put so much effort into empathising and lowering our tone, and regulating our emotions and never getting angry that somewhere along the line we've lost our backbone. We need to find it, and quick.

There are times when we need to be exceptionally and robustly therapeutic. If my children are laughing as I tell them that something they've done is wildly unacceptable, then I raise the tempo and the volume and I plough on like a steam locomotive through and over 'but you said' or a chicken noise or whatever the diversionary tactic is. Some behaviours are unacceptable and that's the end of it, although we have to get skilled at recognising which those are. It can be tempting to interpret lots of behaviours as 'unacceptable' and start throwing our weight around and coming over all punitive and harsh. If we do this, we need to stop. There will be no winners. It's best to take a walk and listen to some Vivaldi instead. I think it's important, though, to be able to recognise when we might be in danger of playing the role of victim, whilst our child, well, I don't really want to say what role they are playing because it's not easy to say. But I will commit to saying that it is our job to model therapeutic assertiveness in the face of abuse, and part of that is not allowing ourselves to be treated like something the dog brought in.

All the good therapeutic work can be done once the flames have died down: exploring feelings, empathising with why they are reacting in this way (the fight of fight/flight/freeze perhaps). One thing's for sure and that is they don't really mean it and they wish they could make it stop too. One technique I've used is to tell them that when I hear the rudeness starting I will tell them I hear it and they have the option of leaving the room and calming down. When the situation arises I will say, 'Remember we talked about this, what would you like to do?' Another technique is to simply say, 'I won't allow myself to be spoken to in this way and so I'm leaving the room.' Another I use is, 'If you want a lift into town later then you'd better stop speaking to me like a piece of crap' whilst getting prepared to follow through. A good reflective exercise to do with them is, 'How would you feel if someone said that to you?' or 'How would you feel if you heard someone else say that to me?' There is always the option which gets right to the heart of the matter, which shouldn't be attempted if we are anywhere near the cliff edge and that is, 'I wonder who it is you are really angry with?'

CHAPTER 7

BROTHERS AND SISTERS

When Mr D. and I decided we would adopt two children our decision process came down to nothing more complicated than simple maths. We knew we wanted two children and we thought that going through the adoption process twice would be annoying and time-consuming. So we applied to adopt siblings. It was as straightforward as that. Little did we know the complexities of parenting two traumatised and related children. It is, I think, the big unspoken about. There is understandably a push to keep sibling groups together, but no one prepares you for the multi-layered challenges that lie ahead when you're the one left holding them together. I guess that social services worry that if there was more honesty around the reality of parenting siblings, then fewer adopters would come forward to do that. I am a simple person. I believe that honesty is the best policy, especially where important, life-changing decisions are concerned. Honesty and better support.

There are of course clear benefits to keeping siblings together. Children grow up not feeling like the odd one out, they have someone around who looks like them and who shares a history with them. But it's not as straightforward as that and trauma can often be the trump card, the card that beats all the others. Developmental trauma results in hard-wired survival strategies which preclude the existence of another in equal need. The brittle voice says, 'I am going to survive at all costs' even if that means standing on a baby brother or sister chick to reach the worm. Some siblings seek to re-enact the traumatic lives they shared. Some children have early experiences of being abused by older siblings in chaotic households where there was little or no adult supervision. The unconditional love we think children should feel towards their siblings is not something I think we should project upon traumatised children.

Our children had never shared a home, and prior to moving in with Mr D. and me had only met up a handful of times before that. They appeared to have little comprehension of what each was to the other. They didn't really know each other and yet there they found themselves sharing a new mum and a new dad and living in a strange new house together. We were all overwhelmed at the time, and looking back, I didn't put enough thought into what it meant to each of them to suddenly have a brother or a sister on top of everything else. That kind of came somewhere near the bottom of the pile in terms of all the other adjustments that needed to take place. And no one really said to us, 'Having a new brother or sister is a massive deal for any child, let alone a traumatised child.' They are expected to feel delighted. We are still dealing with the impact of them not feeling delighted, all these years later. In my view, raising traumatised siblings is vastly under-supported, under-researched and under-discussed. I suspect that it is a factor in adoption breakdown and adoption difficulties. And before some get hot under the collar, I'm not saying that siblings should be separated, I'm just saying that there are more complex and uncomfortable factors that need to be taken into consideration.

As I've said before, children who have cause to doubt that the world is a safe place know love and nurture to be highly conditional and in short supply. The very presence of another child in the family, let alone one who is receiving love and nurture, is a threat to their existence. They will do all they can to put themselves top of the hierarchy of love because it is their best chance of survival. And they will do it by fair means or foul. Mainly foul. They will work out how best to scupper the chances of their sibling in the hierarchy of need and employ all tactics at their disposal. You can try to explain that love is big and endless and can be divided up without being diminished and that it persists despite distance and despite arguments and despite anger and sadness, you can read them all the *To the Moon and Back* books you can lay your hands on, but they will look at you with that expression, that expression that says, 'You have no idea what you're talking about.' And actually most of us don't.

Our children won't be told that there's enough love to go around because that is not their experience of the world. They need to experience bountiful love and nurture over and over and over, and even then their fallback position during times of stress will still be that survival depends on being the last child standing. The brain does not easily give up that which helped it to survive. The problem is that once our children are part of stable and loving families, their survival mechanisms, instead of being of benefit to them, become a great burden, and not only to them but the whole family. However, if there is ever a revolution and times are hard and resources become scarce, I'm sticking with my children because boy they know how to survive.

Apart from the passage of time the most effective measure I've found to help calm sibling rivalry is sharing why it is so rampant in our family. I've shared it gradually and in ways which are appropriate to their understanding and development.

> 'I wonder if the reason you like to get each other into trouble is because you think that that's the way to win love. Is it important to have more love than your sister?'

In our family the straight and unashamed answer will be 'Yes, idiot.' They don't see anything wrong with it at all. And lest anyone want to point out at this point that all siblings compete with each other for love, I know, but please read on. We're talking off the scale here.

'My toothbrush tastes of soap'

'My toothbrush tastes of soap' could also read, 'My phone has disappeared,' 'My favourite Playmobil man has had his hair stolen' or 'Someone has carved a big face into my bed and it definitely wasn't me.'

These are all traps, traps which are laid day after day. The soapy toothbrush one is a classic. The other child may indeed have spread soap on the toothbrush, or the owner may have sabotaged their own toothbrush in order to get the other into trouble. Each is likely. Each has happened. It has been done to goad and to illicit a reaction. It is tempting to fall into the trap and I have done many times. These days I just wash off the toothbrush and say not a word (out loud).

The face carved into the bed is not such an easy one. I am better these days at spotting the body language of the true culprit (and their carving style), and if I am 100 per cent certain who did it then I give a consequence. If I'm not then I employ close supervision for a few days and deliver a pointless lecture about how our home should be a place of safety. I used to get highly agitated when things got gouged and cut, but now I plan a house refurbishment, in about 15 years' time.

> 'He just pinched me on the arm really, really hard,' is another example.

Did he pinch you on the arm really, really hard or did you pinch yourself really, really hard? Again, I only give a consequence when I am quite sure of the events. Sometimes I employ stealth tactics and creep outside a room and observe what is going on. Often I am quite shocked and wish I hadn't, but I think it helps to learn who fabricates and how they appear when they are fabricating. I have actually witnessed a child pinching themselves, shouting, 'Ow, ow, ow' and then crying actual tears and then blaming the other.

Violence between siblings

I once stood at our sitting room window and watched our children playing on the trampoline together. There had been frequent fights and tears but incidents always took place out of my sight, sometimes in the seconds it took me to turn away from them to serve dinner. Our younger child had been telling me for a while that her brother had been hurting her when my back was turned. He denied it outright.

They bounced higher and higher and their laughter got louder. 'How lovely,' I thought until I noticed the eldest trying to trip up the youngest by kicking her legs from under her. She was about eight or nine years old at the time. He eventually succeeded and then prevented her from getting up by jumping closer and closer to her. His laughing moved into the 'hysterical' range and then he stopped jumping and started to kick her. He kicked harder and harder and laughed as he did it and it was like something out of a horrible film. By the time I reached them she was screaming and he was stood with his arms outstretched shouting, 'She hurt me first, I never did anything for God's sake.' He saw my urgency and my anger and ran off shouting, 'You never believe me, you love her more than me.'

In our house, hysterical laughter is an indicator of over-stimulation, loss of control and loss of rational thought and empathy. Risky behaviours often follow close behind.

Your family will no doubt have different dynamics to ours. In ours, the aggressor, following an incident, will act up in a way which demands even more attention than the victim. In fact the aggressor will try to paint himself as the victim ('You don't love me') and it can be so convincing that we can follow the wrong child after an incident. The victim is then left alone to cope with their fear, shock and pain. That can be the way it is for those of us parenting children with different traumas. Leaving the victim alone after such an event is a mistake, I think, and one which I've made too often. It risks teaching the child that they don't deserve comfort, that they are way down in the pecking order, that what happened to them can't have been that bad and that perhaps the way to get attention is to hurt others. If we're not careful then we are playing right into the hands of past trauma and reinforcing old lessons. Going after the aggressor is something I've had to stop myself doing. It is tempting because we have had a big shot of adrenaline and maybe in a state of fight or flight ourselves, especially if the aggressor then becomes aggressive or abusive towards us (or worse still, laughs). There may also be the fear that Red Brain will emerge and things will get out of hand.

The aggressor, pumped up with adrenaline and shame, will probably take flight, but if they fight on, then this is where situations can get out of hand, particularly when there is only one adult around. With two parents at home, in these situations I think that we must take a child each, but it is important that the victim gets a good chunk of time and comfort from the right parent (the parent they are crying for).

There is no template to follow for situations like these. We get to know how our children will react, who is safe to leave for a while and who isn't and where the risks lie. I've had to learn not to panic and that I can afford to take my time, not in breaking up an incident, but in dealing with the fallout and that if I'm not careful I can inflame a situation.

I tell you about the trampoline incident, not because it was the only one of its kind (the 'secret' violence had been taking place for a long time) but because it was a watershed moment for me. It made me look back differently on other incidents and forced me to think much more in terms of past trauma and revictimisation than 'normal' sibling rivalry. We had become habituated and desensitised to acts of violence within our home. Minor incidents became less minor and more frequent and perhaps more secretive. The denials became superbly convincing. The tears are crocodile tears, aren't they? What if they're not? And what if we open our eyes one day and find we are becoming a house where a blind-eye is being turned to violence and we have a child saying, 'My sibling hurts me a lot and I don't tell you because you never believe me and you never do anything about it.'

That's where I found myself, which still unnerves me, because I see myself as a reasonably strong person, with clear values around violence. I can't believe I let it get so bad. But then I was carrying the 'All siblings fight' narrative and not the 'You need to be aware of the risk of inter-sibling violence and rivalry because of your children's early experiences.' I'm not aware of reading or being given any advice about this. It was something else I had to learn for myself.

In shaky moments when self-doubt creeps in I think about what might have happened if I hadn't witnessed the trampoline incident and what the ultimate conclusion could have been. Most likely nothing terrible. But what if a bone had been broken? What then? How would I have explained it? Would the doctor on duty in the A&E Department have known anything about developmental trauma? Perhaps one wouldn't expect them to have this knowledge, but what about the social worker we would have been referred to? Would they? When I talk about sometimes feeling like we live on a knife-edge, this is what I mean, and unless we talk much more openly about the challenges of raising adopted siblings, then taboo subjects like violence will continue to be brushed under the carpet to the disservice of all our children.

Since waking up to the reality of violence in our family I have been able to fall back on the good therapeutic methods that I should have been employing all along. As I mentioned before, my first priority is to make sure everyone is safe. I comfort the hurting child and use phrases such as, 'That must have really hurt' and 'That was totally unacceptable for your brother/sister to do that'. If they will let you comfort them then offer plenty. If they won't (they may put on a convincingly brave face) then I think it is important that we still voice their pain and maybe add,

'I know it is difficult for you to show me that you are hurt.' I
have recently added in, 'No one has a right to treat you like that.'

It is important that the child who did the deed is not left
for too long in shame. No matter what act they put on, they are
likely to be drowning in the stuff. This doesn't take away the
need to state very clearly that it is unacceptable to hurt someone
and this must be said even if they are still protesting innocence
(if they are, I get into steam roller mode and motor through
the denials). It is tempting to get reeled into an argument as
they claim you didn't see the entire incident and so on, but we
mustn't. However, we can still, even in these situations, show
some empathy. I have found the following to be effective:

> 'I've noticed that sometimes when you play with your
> brother/sister you get very excited and lose some control.
> I can hear it coming because your laugh starts to sound
> different (pause whilst denial is voiced but continue on). I'm
> going to be outside with you both when you play together
> and if I think you are losing control then I will step in. I
> will do this because it's my role as a parent to keep you
> both safe.'

Both children will need to be close to an adult for a while. I
would also give a consequence for a big incident such as this. In
our house that might be the child helping me to do something
nice for their sibling, such as putting away their laundry. Some
experts don't advocate giving consequences for poor behaviour,
but in our family this seems to leave a sense of unfinished
business. I don't give them often, but I do for the big stuff.
Something I haven't found of any use, though, is to make the
child apologise. I might during a quiet conversation suggest that
it would be a good thing to do, but I would leave it up to them
and not follow it up. I just don't see the point of ending up in
another stand-off cul-de-sac for something which I'm not sure,
as yet, has a lot of meaning for our children, especially younger
ones. Now that my own children are older they sometimes come

out with spontaneous and heartfelt apologies, which is otherwise known as Progress.

The eyebrows

Traumatised siblings are very skilled at keeping a tally. Even those who struggle with maths and memory can keep up with who sat next to who at the dinner table over the previous six months, who has sat in the front seat of the car more over their lifetime, who had five minutes longer over a bedtime story. It is one of the most tiring aspects of parenting siblings. Nothing is ever for free.

Of course we can understand where this comes from and what fuels it, but that doesn't take away from how frustrating and destructive to family life it can be. I have found this competitive love accountancy personally challenging. Sometimes I wonder if I might just get completely devoured in the fight for love and attention.

You will have your own examples of the things which truly drive you crazy. For me it is the constant arguing over who sits next to me (or if both children are, who can sit the closest), who can hug me for the longest and hardest, who can touch me the most, say 'I love you' the most. If one child perceives that they have the upper hand then they will give the other 'the eyebrows'. 'The eyebrows' is a subtle but irritatingly smug expression which is given in an instant and which is like aiming a flamethrower at a haystack. It is designed to infuriate and it usually works. 'She wants you to react' I will say, 'so try not to'. It doesn't make any difference.

The only practical measure which has helped us is timetabling. Child A will sit in the front seat of the car next to me on outward journeys, Child B will sit next to me on homeward journeys. Mealtimes have had similar arrangements. Mr D. and I take turns taking each child to bed, alternating otherwise there will be terrible going to bed problems ('but Dad took me to bed last night and the night before; you don't want to take me to bed, you don't love me').

As time has gone on and feelings of safety have grown, these behaviours have reduced. They may make a resurgence during times of stress, and when they do, I can usually pin it down to something. Our social worker once advised, 'Say what you see.' It is good advice and I use it when I start to feel I am being wrenched arm from arm:

> 'You both want a lot of me today, and I wonder if that is because you are feeling a bit wobbly about x. You're not? Oh well, I wonder what it might be then.'

I may need to lock myself in the bathroom for ten minutes and scoff chocolate to bring myself down afterwards. Sometimes I might just say, 'For goodness sake you two, stop fighting over me, it's driving me crazy' and walk out. You can't be therapeutic all the time.

'The eyebrows' is something we have given a name to and explored in a comic way, and although this wasn't done with any therapeutic intention, it has definitely taken away some of the sting. Mr D. and I might say, 'Hello eyebrows' when we see them being used, or we might anticipate the use of the eyebrows and say, 'Wait for the eyebrows…' and then we can all laugh about it. 'The eyebrows' make fewer appearances these days.

This is a hijack situation

The ultimate weapon for a child in competition with their brother or sister for love and attention is the hijack. When you really try you can hijack anything. It is particularly effective to hijack good times, because good times are dangerous and scary and conflict with the 'I am bad' of the brittle voice.

Recently I was reading with our daughter in our sitting room. The reading was going well, it was calm and enjoyable. Then our son burst into the room, stood an inch from me and talked loudly, with the aim of disrupting the reading. He couldn't bear to be out in the cold any longer. He sees love as part of a binary system, where the only numbers which exist are 1 and 0. If his sister is getting love that means he has none, so he has to demand it back, so that he has it, but it's just as important that his sister has none.

I could have put money on him disrupting the reading, and what I should have done is talked to him before the reading started and said something like this:

> 'I'm about to read with your sister, and I know that might make you feel that I don't love you. I need you to know that I love you and I'm thinking about you, even when I'm reading with your sister.'

I didn't, because I was tired and because I was already pissed off about something else. That's the way it goes. What I should also have done is reflect back with him:

> 'I notice that you find it hard when your sister reads with me, even though you don't want to read with me. I wonder if you think it means I don't love you as much.'

Many other events are candidates for hijack. Perhaps one child will get an extra day attached to their school holiday. Perhaps a child will be ill and needs to stay off school. Perhaps one has a birthday, or a friend coming round for tea. Each of these common events has to be managed carefully, or sometimes just endured. Often all I can do is point at the school holiday charts which show that EVERYONE GETS THE SAME NUMBER OF DAYS OFF and mutter, 'But I know you find it difficult.' Events like birthdays require a greater amount of stage management. Sometimes one child will go and do something enjoyable with a friend or relative instead of endure (and potentially disrupt) their sibling's party. That's how we have to roll around here.

School can be a particularly tricky source of hijack situations. One child may manage school better than the other. This will not go unnoticed by either. Tales may well get told at home. You may get told, 'He was very naughty at school today, Mummy' or 'Daddy you would have been very cross if you knew what she did in assembly.' It is very difficult not to take the bait. I've taken it plenty of times and regretted it. My motto is, 'What happens at school, stays at school.' Our children now attend different schools and always will. This separation has taken a whole lot of conflict out of the equation and has benefited us all.

Ganging up

Despite pretending to hate each other's guts, when the chips are down there can be no stronger allies nor more intimidating opponents than two siblings united, bound together by fear and trauma. At least that's my experience. I haven't ever read about this phenomenon or heard anyone else describe it, so I could be imagining it (I'm not), or it is unique to our family of adopted siblings (surely not?).

Anyway, it goes something like this. School holidays. You are looking after both children. Your partner is at work (lucky partner). Child A has been troubled by something and is displaying that kind of jerky, spiky, semi-out-of-control behaviour that might lead to something serious. You comfort Child A despite being told to 'eff off' or whatever. Child B stays close, feeling unnerved by the behaviour and expressing that the verbal abuse, or kicking, or whatever being displayed is wrong. Child A appeals to Child B with zany behaviour to cross the border and side against you. What fun it would be. Both start to shows signs of hysteria. Child B suddenly finds Child A's behaviour funny and allegiances change. You are facing a mutiny. No amount of 'calm but firm' works. You raise your voice, put on your serious face and are mocked. They run rings around you. They start to raise the stakes. Now they are going to pack their bags and run away. They go in different directions manically throwing food and toys into bags. They laugh. It is a different kind of laugh. It is out of control and chilling. They try to climb out of windows, reach for keys to unlock doors. They declare they will break windows and climb out. They search for heavy objects and start to bash them against glass. Your attempts to lock doors and secure keys attract more excitement and manic laughter. 'What are you going to do now, Mummy?' someone will say with a jeer and a sneer, 'go and cry to Daddy, boo hoo, like that, you little weakling.' You have officially lost control.

Now, we've all been told often enough that one must never shout at adopted children with developmental trauma and attachment issues. It is great advice, but I don't always follow it. With all the techniques I've been taught and practised and used to great effect, the only thing which breaks through this kind of madness is proper, loud, in control, sergeant-major style SHOUTING.

> 'I'm in charge here, not you. Now you (and I will I'm afraid pick on the more malleable one here, it is important to break the alliance as soon as possible by way of divide and conquer) sit there, SIT THERE, NOW.'

My voice will be so loud and so insistent that it shocks perhaps not both, but one child out of the collective madness. I will then continue:

> 'Whether you like it or not, you are part of this family and you are not, I repeat, NOT leaving it.'

There may be an attempt to butt in here to try to divert, but I raise the volume and keep going (it is important not to show any wavering, any weakness). When I feel that the atmosphere has changed sufficiently that real danger of mutiny has passed, I start to address the desire to run away. I will explore where they were going to go, where they would sleep and what they would eat. I would empathise with the desire, but also point out the challenges of sleeping on top of the climbing frame at the park or in the neighbour's shed. Wherever this takes us, it is important to try to voice where all this has come from, and that is fear.

> 'I wonder if you think we are going to send you away and so you want to leave first. I can understand that because in your experience you have been rejected and that's really, really tough. All I can say is that you are my children forever, through all the good times and the tough.'

The chances are that the 'quieter' sibling will be left wondering how they got caught in this tide of insurrection. Whenever this has happened I wonder aloud with them and away from their sibling. I will use the narrative technique to show that I understand this was out of character for them and that they may have scared themselves, and what they may want to do to protect themselves if it happens again.

After a big incident like this there will usually be a period of quiet and stunned shock and perhaps crying and hugging. I think that a lot of valuable work can be done during this time to show that we love them and care for them through thick and thin. They seem particularly open in this state, and for that reason showing nurture and love and not anger and distance is important (but not always humanly possible).

These incidents have been few and far between in our family, but their impact is enormous and I will never forget them. The decreasing frequency is partly down to maturity and partly to understanding that no matter what, we are a family that is sticking together. Permanence is the ultimate message of love and healing.

Differing 'trauma styles'

Siblings may feel very differently about their pasts and express their trauma differently from each other. Some just can't hide their trauma and are all out there and angry and shouting, whereas others are more ashamed and secretive and uncomfortable with the whole thing. I've called the differing ways in which our children show their trauma 'trauma styles'. I've made it up. Or at least I think I have. I've read so many books and been on so many courses it could have come from anywhere. If it's your phrase then I hope you don't mind if I borrow it for a while.

There are benefits to parenting children with different trauma styles. There are also drawbacks. It is something I wrestle with every single day of the week. It is the 'but' which comes into one's mind on hearing about a cracking technique for parenting a child with trauma. It is the thick layer of complexity inside the therapeutic parenting cake.

Helping a child to process trauma is a delicate and careful exercise in patience and empathy. It has to be done but at the right pace. March ahead too quickly and we risk the child being overwhelmed. Shy away and the trauma can become more secretive and locked in. This is the tightrope that many of us walk, learning, reading our children and adjusting our approaches as we go along. Having two or more children in the family with developmental trauma can mean that the foot goes on the accelerator too hard for too long for one, or the brakes are applied so the thing moves too slowly for the other.

Adjusting our therapeutic parenting styles so that all our children are understood and best served is not easy. We can appear to be inconsistent and unfair. We can find ourselves parenting to the lowest common denominator. The only way through all this is to be open, and like the good social worker said to me, 'Say what you see.'

I've got better at explaining why I sometimes parent our two children differently from each other, why boundaries are fair in the broad sense, but take account of individual difficulties and priorities, but it isn't easy.

The Trauma See-Saw

You may not experience the Trauma See-Saw in your house. In our house it is Trauma See-Saw all the way. There is very little 'balance' or stasis.

I have made up the term Trauma See-Saw because I don't know how else to describe it and I haven't read about the phenomenon anywhere (I haven't read much about raising traumatised siblings anywhere). The process, in my experience, goes something like this:

> Child A has a patch of anger and aggression and bloody-mindedness. It sends the family into turmoil. Before you know it Child A is the focus of everyone's attention. They are definitely 'up in the air'.
>
> Meanwhile Child B is terribly compliant and polite and helpful. They shake their head at the antics of Child A and may even commiserate with you over how hard it is to parent them. They are 'down on the ground'.
>
> Child A starts to make progress and the anger and aggression and bloody-mindedness slowly diminish. It feels as though they are emerging from behind a cloud and coming out into the sunshine. They start to move down to ground level.
>
> For a moment both children are in equilibrium. It is wonderful. You start to plan things, like foreign holidays and trips to West End theatres. You find yourself saying, 'Things are so much better'. This is a terrible error, one which I have made countless times. Touching something made of wood offers no protection at all from the forces of the Trauma See-Saw.
>
> Suddenly the normally quiet and compliant Child B becomes demanding and contrary. Then Child B becomes rude and cuts holes in things you like. Child

B becomes very difficult indeed. Child B is 'up in the air' and you've barely had time to recover your energies.

Meanwhile Child A is so terribly sweet and helpful and you suspect is almost enjoying the turmoil being experienced by Child B. They have entirely swapped places.

You may not have a Trauma See-Saw in your house, or it may be a different process altogether, like Trauma British Bulldog, or Trauma Tag. I tell you about Trauma See-Saw because it took me ages to work out that this what was going on, and once I'd worked it out it made sense. It is an analogy that I share with our children to help them understand what's going on.

Although there is a certain relentlessness to the Trauma See-Saw, there are some benefits to it too. Taking turns to express and then process trauma gives each child some time off. To be in full-blown trauma the whole time would be exhausting and damaging. To take it in turns makes sense. There is also the matter of the 'down on the ground' child being able to witness what 'up in the air' looks like from a distance. As they get older our children might start to say, 'Is that what I'm like when I'm angry?' or 'You handled that well, Mum.'

If Trauma See-Saw doesn't fit your family, then maybe make up your own analogy, if you have the energy and the headspace. But whatever you do, don't go touching any 'lucky' wood.

Family therapist-in-training

Our older child is so well-versed in the therapeutic approach now that he can act as a very able 'wing man' during times of crisis. I don't want to be too boastful, but his skills in that department are advanced beyond some professionals I've come across. These skills don't always show themselves, but when the chips are down, boy is he amazing.

'I know how scary it feels to be out-of-control angry.'

'Mum is doing the right thing to keep you safe.'

'It is important to let your feelings out because if they stay locked inside it isn't good.'

'I know you didn't mean it but you said some mean things and you should apologise for that.'

He is empathetic without having to try. He is wise and practical. He helps me understand the approaches which work against those which don't.

Just as one example, when something loud is going down and shoes and insults are being thrown, he tells me that he finds it very triggering to listen to it from another room. He feels much safer if he can sit alongside me. Just knowing that makes a difference to how I do things.

In the same situation our younger child will support by bringing tissues or a drink and will stroke an arm or offer a hug.

Living with a brother or sister with trauma is hard, but it is not all bad news. Witnessing a sibling's anger or anxiety can give a child a window on to how they themselves are feeling and acting. There is no harm in that 'Goodness, is that what I'm like?' moment as long as it is supported with acceptance and empathy.

CHAPTER 8

THE OUTSIDE WORLD

Living inside the pressure-cooker of family life is hard, but it is only once we step out of our front door that the challenges really kick in. The outside world is set to 'normal', and everyday experiences of family life like friendships, going to school, going shopping or trying to access support can all highlight the fact, in glorious detail, that many of us are not operating on the normal scale. Like it or not our families are different from most other people's and some just don't understand that at all.

I try to maintain empathy for those who lack understanding, although it is hard. I wonder how understanding I'd have been if I'd had a run-of-the-mill family. I can't say with certainty that I'd have behaved with total compassion. I can say, however, that I wouldn't have been a totally offensive clot.

General knowledge around attachment issues and developmental trauma is definitely increasing, and in the years I've been a parent I've noticed an improvement. However, there are still enormous, drafty gaps. If you find yourself feeling the draft, whether that's amongst family and friends, or at school or within the health system, then you have my sympathy. Being an adopter can feel a bit like being a one man or one woman preacher of a fringe religion. Not only do we live with the fallout of trauma, we have to try to convince the world that it is a real thing. Sometimes I imagine that the journalist John Sweeney is making a shock documentary about me and is staking out my house with a camera crew, and then I get doorstepped and he shouts in my face that I'm a crazy fantasist. Then I go on an adoption course or meet up with a friend in the same situation and am reminded that I'm not a basket case (quite yet).

Insensitive questions and comments

I wanted to call this section 'Rude fools' but I'm not sure I'll get away with it so I'll stick with 'Insensitive questions and comments' for now. But really, some people are so very rude. If you've come to adoption via the cul-de-sac of infertility, then you will have met them already. They are not always who you think they'll be.

Insensitive questions and comments are usually uttered by the psychopathically nosey, and include gems like:

'Couldn't you have your own children?'

'I'd have loved to adopt but…'

'Did you try IVF?'

'It's marvellous what you've done.'

'Those children are so lucky.'

'What happened to them?'

'How did he get that scar on his arm?'

I've found that these are generally the types of people who cultivate their tendency to speak before they think as though it is an extremely funny and endearing personality trait, when in fact it is just plain offensive. Who knows what internal struggles they're battling with? (Actually I don't care.)

Did you know that every time a foolish adoption myth is repeated, the great Adoption Klaxon is sounded? Yes, in my head, perhaps in yours too. You will have a long list of your own favourite adoption myths, but here are mine, just for darkly comic purposes:

'They were so young they won't remember anything.'

'Children are very resilient.'

'All they need is love.'

'All they need is firm boundaries.'

'All children do that.' (My personal favourite.)

'They'll grow out of it.'

'You need to tell him that's wrong.'

'I expect you find it difficult to work out what is due to their past and what is just normal.' (Answer: no.)

'It is hard being a parent even to birth children you know.' (Only possible answer: f**k you.)

Oh yes, when it comes to brain science and child psychology everyone's an expert. I'm afraid I have no magic solution to offer you. Most of the time I grit my teeth and swear offensively in my head, then I go home and bash household objects together. It mostly works for me for the day-to-day passing comment. It doesn't work so well when faced with institutionalised stupidity.

School

Pressure upon children to enjoy school, to love learning and to excel academically comes at them from all sides. When asked by some well-meaning adult if he likes school our son will simply reply 'no'. It is always clear it was not the answer the questioner was expecting. Educational wonderfulness is our measure of a marvellous child, and these days there are no excuses. All children are expected to finish school with a clutch of the right kind of GCSEs, free school lunches or no free school lunches, and schools are judged on their ability to make this happen.

On the face of it a good education tools up disadvantaged children for a bright future, and yet many adoptive families report that school comes top of their list of things that keep them awake at night. At worst school can be something that puts unbearable strain on family life.

Many of us come to realise what the experts in child trauma and attachment have long spoken about, and that is that secure attachments and emotional health have to be put before SATs and GCSEs and the like if children and young people are to have any hope of living happy and fulfilling lives. I haven't come to this conclusion because I am a flaky liberal, but because of one glaringly obvious (to me, in any case) fact: frightened, traumatised children don't learn. In education-speak, trauma and attachment problems are barriers to learning. Great big ones. Worse than that, they cause children to forget things they once knew and to lose skills they had once gained. In a knot of frustration I once took a story into school which our son had written at home. It was fabulous. His teacher was gobsmacked. How could he be capable of such brilliance at home but not at school, she wondered? It must be that he was just conning everyone at school into thinking he was stupid. Overnight he changed from being the stupid child to the one who wasn't putting his back into things.

My experience has helped me to reach the understanding that unless children feel safe, accepted and understood at school they may as well not be there. I know that this will bring on gasps of horror, but that's where I've ended up, and believe me it's a long way away from where I started. Secure attachments, a strong positive sense of worth and hope for the future form the springboard from which young people can make a life for themselves, whether that's by making the most that education can offer them, or by other means. A child who has not benefited from all that secure early care gives is severely disadvantaged.

There is (prepare for another gasp) plenty of time for GCSEs and A-levels because those boats offer more than one sailing. But ignore a child or a young person's needs for good attachment experiences and emotional health and we risk sending them out into the world without the necessary skills to build healthy relationships and to make sound choices.

Whilst a lot of good work gets done within the family, it can all be obscured if we send our child off to a school every day where they feel scared, triggered and their emotional reactions are misinterpreted as 'naughty'. Once a child is identified by others and identifies themselves as 'naughty', all the good therapeutic work carried out at home to help our children to experience themselves as inherently good is pissed into the wind. Punishing them for not being able to focus, for being 'silly' or angry, is as good as saying, 'You're absolutely right, you are a bad child and you deserve all you get.' Really we've got to be cleverer than to play into the hands of trauma like this.

My own children have had some less than great experiences of school but are now doing fair to well. School has been a generator of relentless anguish *and* it has been a source of fantastic support and great teaching. It can be done well and it is important that it is done well.

I was entirely under-prepared for everything that 'school' in its broadest sense would throw at us, and like so much of adoptive parenting, I've learned this the hardest, steepest, muddiest way, so for what it's worth, here's what I wish I'd known ten years ago.

Choosing a school

Choosing a school for our child is one of the most crucial decisions we make as adoptive parents. As many of our children find school a particularly challenging part of life, I think it's best to be prepared for this. If they sail through school, at least it will come as a nice surprise.

Our eldest child started school soon after he was placed with us. To say that I was naive about the possible pitfalls of school would be an understatement. What I really needed was someone to sit alongside me, to help me choose a school and support me in easing our son's transition into full-time education. At the time all anyone wanted to say was, 'I expect he'll be fine.' He wasn't. If I'd known then what I know now I'd have gone about the business of choosing a school very differently.

Here is a list of things you might want to consider when choosing a school for your child:

- Shop around. Go to school open days and talk to staff. Pretend that you are interviewing schools for the privilege of teaching your child. Don't do what I did and assume that the nearest school will do just fine.

- Read the latest Ofsted report but don't assume that the school with the highest grade will necessarily be the most suitable for your child. Pay particular attention to how the school rates in its support of children with additional needs.

- Visit a wide range of schools, especially if you are unfamiliar with the school environment as I was. Start to get a feel for how they differ in resources, approach and general atmosphere.

- Keep an open mind about what size of school will best suit your child. A small school may offer a greater sense of safety and nurture, but a child with 'emotional and behavioural difficulties' can stand out and find it harder to make friends, particularly if that school is in (now how can I put this?) a more 'middle-class' area. A larger school may be busier and noisier, but more diverse and have more resources available to support children with additional needs.

- Talk to parents who have children at the school, particularly those with experience of additional needs, and ask them about their experiences.

Once you have narrowed your choice down, ask to look around the school. Write a list of questions. Here are some suggestions:

- Explain that your child is placed for adoption with you, or has been adopted by you and is likely to find school more challenging than other children. What reaction do staff give? If you hear anything like 'He/she will be fine,' 'They just need love and a firm routine' or anything else which sets off the Adoption Klaxon, then alarm bells should be ringing. If, on the other hand, staff take you seriously and show knowledge and experience of attachment difficulties and developmental trauma, then this is a good sign.

- Has the school supported adopted or fostered children before? What support was put in place for them?

- How flexible will the school be in allowing your child a gradual introduction to school? It is important to bear in mind that our children can be developmentally younger than their peers and may not be ready for full-time education. A child who is hyper-alert to danger will tire more easily than their peers and may be exhausted after a few hours at school.

- Ask about the school's behaviour policy. Is it weighted towards sanctions or rewards? How public are any systems in place? Are there charts on the walls recording children's behaviour? How shaming might a behaviour system be to a child with chronically low self-esteem? Do children miss out on fun activities if they've been 'naughty'? Worse still, do they have to watch the other children taking part in the fun activity as punishment? It is important to remember and for school to be aware that adopted children often believe themselves to be bad and worthless, and some behaviour systems may reinforce this negative self-image (aka 'making things worse').

- What is the school's policy for excluding or suspending a child from school? Has this sanction been used over the past 12 months, and if so, for what reason? Be wary of schools which seem 'trigger happy' when it comes to exclusions. Our children need to know that the adults around them are in it for the long haul and accept them for who they are.

- Get a feel for whether the school is highly results-driven. If it is, that's not necessarily a bad thing as long as the nurture and support are in place as well. Success is different for different children.

- Ask about the provision of attachment figures and rooms for children to go to if they are struggling to cope with lessons (this will really test the levels of knowledge and experience about attachment and trauma).

- Ask how flexible the school will be if your child finds particular aspects of school such as PE, school trips and lunchtimes difficult. Do they have the ability to lay on additional supervision if necessary?

- Ask whether your child might be eligible for funding for additional support.

- Ask how much homework your child will be expected to do. Is the school keen on homework or does it believe that it is inappropriate for younger children? How flexible are they willing to be on the level of homework your child will be expected to do? If you have young children then you may not yet know the homework delights that await you. Homework is a bloody nightmare in most adoptive families, and I say this from horrible experience.

- Would the school be prepared to work in partnership with you to achieve the best for your child? Would they be prepared to read information on attachment and developmental trauma if they haven't already? Would they be prepared to meet with other professionals involved with your child such as social workers?

- Have staff received any training in attachment issues and education?

- What is your 'gut feel' of the school? Were you made to feel welcome? Did staff listen to you?

Being a strong advocate

Before ducking out of corporate life and seeking refuge in heritage gardening, I spent a lot of my time at work negotiating. I negotiated with suppliers and customers (and occasionally some jobsworth in charge of stationery requisitions or meeting-room bookings), and the emphasis was on long-term relationships. From the outside the job of a negotiator can seem a hard and uncompromising one, but this is far from reality. The art of negotiation is about reaching a conclusion that is satisfactory to all parties, because if you steal a win, you won't the next time. Good negotiations are based on trust and on each party understanding the needs and motivations of the other. I used to come across the table-thumping type of negotiator and invariably they were inexperienced and unconfident and trying to compensate for that by being shouty and aggressive (and much like a bully, coming from a place of weakness). The problem came when they would later need to call in a favour and there were none in the bank.

As advocates of children who need something extra from the education system we can't afford to be meek about it, neither can we afford to go around thumping tables and burning bridges. In short, we need to behave like experienced negotiators. Experienced negotiators don't view the others around the table as the enemy, but as normal and likeable people, much like they are, but with a different job to do. That's the headspace we need to get in to.

Our own experience of the education system has been varied and is now good. At the start I might have been Mrs Naive of Wishful Thinking Street, but I'm not anymore. I no longer stumble into meetings in shock, then apologise and cry. I have come to realise that there's an art to being a good advocate. Here are some of the things I've learned.

- Look well-presented. It shouldn't matter what we look like, but it does. I dress like a smarter version of myself, so I feel comfortable and confident (even if I'm not feeling it).

- Be well-prepared. Write down exactly what you want to discuss and do the background reading. Write down phrases you might want to use so you can fall back on them if you need to. Bring books with you that show you know what you're talking about and which give credence to attachment issues and developmental trauma.

- Put on a cloak of confidence.

- Try your very best not to cry or to get angry. If you are in a bad place then consider rescheduling the meeting, writing a letter instead, or bringing a social worker or someone else who can support you to the meeting. I have learnt this from bitter experience.

- Always be polite. Most professionals are doing their best but just might not know enough about attachment and trauma, yet. They may well set the Adoption Klaxon sounding, as many people without knowledge of trauma do. It's all right to gently correct. Something like, 'Although that is the received opinion, it's not what modern research is telling us' might be more helpful than, 'What an idiotic and patronising thing to say.' Anger and frustration is best expressed in the confines of our homes (or in my case, occasionally on social media).

- Foster relationships. If you come across a member of staff who really gets attachment and trauma issues, then embrace them (perhaps not literally). Tell them how much you appreciate their support and understanding. Buy them chocolates at Christmas. Compliment good practice. Many members of staff don't hear the words 'thank you' very often.

- Share your child's history. If teachers are expected to understand and support our children, then I think they deserve to know why our child presents in the way they do. This is a partnership after all. I'm not saying that we go sharing private information hither and thither, but within reason. Knowing about a child's background can also help nurture empathy: one of the key ingredients in the educational flapjack.

- Gently remind. We all lose sight of why our children operate in the way they do during times of stress. I do and sometimes I need reminding. It is the same for teaching staff. Part of our job as advocates is to keep our child's history in everyone's minds so that it informs how we respond to them. Sometimes I might say something like, 'I wonder if that approach might have made him feel shame' (the 'I wonder' approach works for adults as well as children I've found), or 'Perhaps *we* need to find a different way of dealing with this.' It's the non-confrontational, non-accusatory stuff that works best.

- Introduce the language of attachment and trauma. By using terms like 'hyper-vigilant' rather than 'easily distracted' and 'hyper-stimulated' rather than 'over-excitable and silly' around school we nudge others to a more professional and compassionate approach to our child. Language shapes our perceptions and words matter.

- Pick your battles. Some parents just can't help themselves from being perpetual complainers. They are forever confronting the teacher in the playground about reading schemes or why there isn't more homework, or why their child hasn't been picked for the football team. They don't shy away from moaning to other parents too, sometimes whipping up an ego-driven mini-tornado of dissatisfaction which rumbles around the school playground for months. Teachers get very tired of these sorts of parents. It is for this reason that we must focus on the important issues and play the long game.

- Keep school informed. If your child has had a meltdown over some homework, or hasn't been able to read every night, let the school know. This can avoid your child getting into trouble and can raise awareness that your child is going through a particularly difficult time.

- Have regular reviews. We have termly reviews at both our children's schools which help everyone to refocus on the important things. We talk about everything the child finds challenging about school and ways in which they can be supported. Actions are taken and followed up. The atmosphere is open, supportive and thinking is creative. These meetings have made a big difference to our children's success at school.

- Set realistic expectations. Early on in our children's education I expected too much of them, and sometimes I still do. I paid too much attention to what other children were achieving. What I know now is that education is a long process, and many of our children start from a point of severe disadvantage. Sometimes success is getting to school, wearing a school uniform, nothing more.

- Be brave. If the school is lacking in empathy and support for your child despite all your best and protracted efforts, then it may be time to consider moving on. It is not a measure to be taken lightly, but it can be a game-changer. It has been for our family.

Good practice

Our elder child does not particularly enjoy school and finds it a difficult environment to be in. There have been times when

I've wondered if he will be able to stay in school at all until 16, let alone achieve anything. That's all shifted now that he is in the right school and broadly has the right support around him. School is still not his number one most favourite place in the world, but he goes and he functions reasonably well and is making progress. There are a number of measures and features of his school which have made all the difference to him. Many of them have been learnt from Louise Bomber's books and training courses, which I strongly recommend.

- Willingness of staff to continue learning effective ways of supporting adopted and fostered children by reading books and going on courses.

- 'Therapeutic' methods within school are modelled by those at the top of the organisation and reflected through the school. It isn't just seen as a specialisation for those who work in student support.

- An ability to hear 'the brittle voice' and to see behaviours as symptoms of trauma and not wilful 'naughtiness'. Children who cannot sit still, who cannot keep quiet, who call out, who scribble on their books are only responding to the world in ways which they have learnt keeps them alive. They are little balls of hyper-alert stress, and that stress seeps out of them. I think it's best to let it seep in an accepting way, rather than try to force them to hold it in. Quiet and very compliant children may in some ways be easier to teach, but they are the swans of the classroom: all calm above water, but paddling like billy-o underneath. They have a brittle voice too, and it is quiet but still has to be heard. Children who hold on to their stress at school can let it all flood out at home in ways which those who are not familiar with trauma could never dream of. If we are aiming for a foundation of emotional health and security from which to start building an education, then we need to avoid this bunching up and spilling out of stress as far as we can.

- A real understanding of why behaviour systems which may work for other children may not work for adopted children. For example, behaviour systems which involve public shaming or which are long-lasting may just teach a child already well-acquainted with shame that they are indeed bad and everything is their fault. My experience is that the teachers who have helped our children to make the best progress are those who focus on their relationships with them first. Children who experience teachers as punitive can give up on trying to please them and may even see the classroom as a battleground. When it gets that bad, all is close to lost. Rather counter-intuitively the same can go for rewards and praise. The most effective rewards are small and quiet, not loud and demonstrative. The small and quiet rewards gently chip away at shame, the loud and demonstrative ones try to pretend it doesn't exist, which, as we know, is a flawed approach.

- Flexibility of thinking and a willingness to try out different strategies. For example, reducing the length of the school day or the school week for adopted children, putting in place additional support during lunch and break times, reducing amounts of homework, not forcing them to take part in activities they cannot cope with.

- Putting in place an attachment figure. An attachment figure is like a mum or a dad at school. It is someone the child knows and likes and feels safe with. They are the safe harbour during a storm. They are the person who says, 'I've been thinking about you' and 'Would you like a Malteser?' and 'I understand that maths is difficult for you.' For younger children this needs to be someone who is around every day and who spends some one-to-one time with them, getting to know them and enjoying their company. Older children, even big, strapping adolescents, still need an attachment figure at school. The presence of an attachment figure for me is one of the most important strategies to have in place. This person can also act as an efficient communication channel between home and school. I can email our child's attachment figure and tell her we are having a difficult time at home and she will make sure she finds our son at school and chats to him and generally 'checks in'. We coordinate many aspects of school between us and she has been a great support to me.

- Significant adults is something I have made up, but in my experience their presence around school supports the work of an attachment figure. These members of staff are those who 'get' your child and like them, and may not have gone within ten miles of a training course in attachment and schools. They are those naturally funny and caring PE teachers and art teachers and receptionists who help to populate our child's world with positive experiences. It's not easy to identify these individuals, but as the school years roll on, they gradually make themselves known and we can make contact with them, if only to say 'thank you' every now and again.

- Helping the child to feel safe at school is particularly important for children who transition from a small to a larger school. Explaining a school's security systems can ease a troubled mind. Our son was scared of strangers who were in the school grounds so the signing-in book and pass system were explained and the fence around the school was explored. These measures may need to be repeated over and over.

- Having a safe place to go in school is important for our children. It may not be the place that we'd like it to be. It may be the room the teaching assistants go in to have their coffee, it may be the library, or it may be the year head's office. Wherever it is, if a child seeks out comfort then they should be welcomed. It is a big step for them to seek comfort and safety at school, so it should be seen as a step in the right direction.

- A 'Time-Out' card (or as I've seen it described in a letter from school a 'Get Out of Jail Free' card) is perhaps the one strategy which ties everyone's pants in knots. In my experience it is an essential part of the toolkit. When a child is starting to feel out of control, instead of staying in a lesson and causing disruption and getting into trouble in front of the entire class, they show the card and, without fuss from anyone, quietly leave the room and go to their safe place. When they feel calm enough to return to lessons, they do. When this system was first introduced with our son I was worried that he'd use it all the time, to avoid lessons he didn't like. The opposite has been true. He has needed to be encouraged, because he doesn't want to appear to be different from the other children, but now he is much better at reading his own emotions and deciding when he needs to leave the classroom. So much about supporting our children is teaching them coping strategies, and this is a really important one. So, if your child is frequently disrupting lessons and failing, then I would put on your cloak of confidence and suggest to school that they dust off their laminating machine.

- Ability to see beyond the immediate problems and towards the long view. Not being panicked and not reacting to 'the small stuff' is so important. As I've mentioned before, success is sometimes a whole different thing for our children. For some children success is continuing to live with their adoptive family, not how many GCSEs they get.

- An ability to react in a therapeutic yet robust way when situations demand. There may be times when a more traditional approach is required, but it should still be delivered with empathy and understanding. I'm thinking here of those more serious misdemeanours which need a clear message attached to them.

- Working in partnership with parents is essential. Warning parents when something major has happened at school, keeping parents informed about progress and actions, holding regular meetings, really committing to a two-way conversation are what will help to keep the show on the road.

- School is rarely ever close to a perfect experience for many of our children. I think it's best to accept that it won't be perfect and work on what is achievable. So much of our children's success is based upon whether they like their teachers or not. For example, I have just filled in a GCSE options form which is entirely based around which teachers are 'nice' and which ones are 'horrible'.

The most important part of the support at school for our family has been the desire for staff to learn about supporting children with attachment difficulties and developmental trauma in school. They have read books and been on courses, listened and learned. And they report that many of the therapeutic methods work well with 'normal' children as well. Bingo.

Getting help – a short rant

I wish that this was the section of the book where I could celebrate the marvellous wrap-around service, the superb therapeutic support, the knowledgeable and compassionate professionalism that is available to support all our families. I wish that there had been no need for me to write this book at all.

Forgive me if I am blunt for a moment. The service provided to traumatised, adopted children and their families in the UK is, at the time of writing, generally appallingly terrible. Of course this isn't universally true. There are pockets of good practice. I can't be any more positive than this, and I say this as a glass half full kind of a person.

In the UK therapeutic support for children who have experienced the worst of times falls to a part of the NHS called Child and Adolescent Mental Health Services (CAMHS). CAMHS is often referred to as a 'Cinderella Service'. I've even heard it called this within NHS commissioning circles. I've also heard it spoken about as the building no one wants to work in, the field where the lame horses are put out to grass for their last few years of unsteady life, the café in the crappy part of town with the grubby tables and the chipped coffee cups. Everyone knows it is poorly resourced and under-powered.

You may be lucky enough to live in an area with a strong CAMHS capability and a short waiting list. You may, like me, live in an area where CAMHS does not have the expertise or the capacity to support adoptive families at all. It is, it seems, acceptable for families in desperate need of help (families who have, let's not forget, adopted children from the care of the state) to be turned away. It is the stuff of poor and under-developed countries and I wouldn't have believed it could happen in a modern economy like ours unless I had experienced it myself. If the NHS was refusing to treat children and young people with heart problems or broken limbs it would be headline news. People would lose their jobs. Questions would be asked in the House.

For about a year Mr D. and I took part in a pilot project which extended therapeutic support on offer to some foster carers, to adopters. I wrote about it in my first book *No Matter What*. It made a significant difference to our family life and I would go so far as to say that without that support we may not have held our family together. This service is no longer provided at all in our area, except privately (if you're lucky). If I had a magic wand I would make this kind of service available to all adoptive families who need it.

Helpful help and unhelpful help

Simplistically speaking, there are, in my experience, two types of help: helpful help and unhelpful help. As adopters we need to get good at quickly spotting which is which.

Unhelpful help can make matters a whole lot worse than they already are. I have learnt to be careful which professionals I let into the lives of my children. I don't have the time or the energy to waste on pursuing the wrong help, and our children certainly don't need the stress of yet another ham-fisted intervention. I've learnt that unless a professional knows about trauma and attachment, there is little point getting involved with them. The wrong kind of intervention can be worse than no intervention at all.

If a professional sets off the Adoption Klaxon then my suspicions are immediately awakened. If they question my experience, judgement or sanity, or seek to blame me in any way, then I back out of the room. Developmental trauma and attachment issues are real things. There are plenty of professionals out there who 'get' trauma and who can make a significant difference, but sadly it's not always that easy to get access to them. If I want crappy, blamey advice then frankly I'll just go and stand at a bus stop and chat to random strangers.

Likewise, if a professional looks at you like you are some kind of a hysteric when you use the language of attachment and trauma, then be wary. If they suggest that you need the types of parenting classes that people with zero parenting skills get told to go on, then smile politely and forget to make another appointment (this is what I've done before). Our children need a different kind of parenting: therapeutic parenting (which this book is about).

When things are so bad that we, the parents, feel traumatised, we lose the ability to explain what life is like, the day-to-day hideousness of it, the dread of waking up in the morning. We become lost for words. This disables us in the quest to find helpful help, and can make it appear as though the problem is ours, that we are mentally deficient. My advice, offered from the sting of experience, is don't waste your time convincing others if they don't want to hear. Find an unlocked door to push on instead. There are some around, although there should be many more.

Just as an aside (because this is getting a bit heavy and depressing and there is more than enough of that to be going along with) here's a funny (stroke) depressing thing. You, like us, may have had cause to see many different medical professionals during the course of your family life. It comes with the territory. We have seen our GP and health visitor, speech and language therapists, a paediatrician, our dentist and a consultant orthodontist. Two out of this list have displayed knowledge and appreciation of the issues around trauma and attachment difficulties in children and have delivered the most compassionate and brilliant treatment. Guess which they were? Yep, funny, and yet depressing.

You will know when you have found the right kind of help. You will not have to explain or justify yourself. You will hear things like, 'I know how hard that must be' and 'I've worked with plenty of families and I can help.' As well as empathy so warm it will make you want to melt into a pool of your own tears, there will be practical tips and suggestions that actually work. Many of the tips will chime with what you know from your reading and the training courses you have been on and with your real, lived, often baffling experience. You will feel able to admit your mistakes in the knowledge that you will not be blamed. There will be a patience and understanding and hope. There will be, at the core of 'helpful help', an understanding that the key to helping our children heal is to encourage and nurture our relationships with them. There will be none of this 'I need to work with/talk to your child without you there.' The best support and advice, in my opinion, is about teaching us, the number one people in our child's lives, how to create the environment in which our child feels safe enough to take our hand and start on the journey of healing and growing. Much of the best therapeutic intervention Mr D. and I experienced took place whilst our children were at school, oblivious to all the good work that was taking place.

Friends and family

During our adoption preparation Mr D. and I were asked to draw a network of the friends and family members who would support us in parenting our, at that time, unknown adopted children. With a few exceptions we got it quite wrong.

Like bereavement, adopting children, especially those with 'issues', shows you who your real friends are. I found this realisation very hard indeed. During the worst times I wondered if I had any friends at all.

Some of those friendships petered out because I had been propping them up and could no longer. They had a limited life and were going to end at some point. Others faltered because babies arrived and time and energy was scarce. There were friendships, however, that withered because we had our children through adoption.

I have always tried to be thoughtful when others have had babies. I have sent presents in the post, some of them I even I knitted myself. When our children arrived, apart from gifts from close family members, we only received things from my very best friend and some neighbours of my parents. I tried not to take it personally at the time, but failed. In truth I felt forgotten and lonely when I was least equipped to dealing with feeling like that.

Part of this is because people don't know what to do or say when someone they know adopts a child. There is no script to follow, and so instead of making mistakes the subject is avoided until it becomes too difficult to regain contact. I get that.

As we get older our friendships change. Perhaps adoption just speeds up the process.

At the same time as building a family I found myself having to build friendships too. I did it eventually and now have a strong circle of friends who I rely on a lot, but it took an amount of strength and confidence on my part which were in short supply at the time. Some older friendships have been rekindled now that our children are older and we have more time to ourselves. These are mostly long-distance relationships which are more difficult to nurture anyway.

What I didn't expect was to form new friendships with other adopters. This has been a lovely surprise and has made it all worth it. Adoption changes us significantly and for the better I believe, and it is enriching to know others who are going through the same process.

I tell you this in case you find yourself in the same boat as I was. It seems to be a common experience. It's not a great feeling to admit we have few friends and to face weeks of summer holidays with no playdates. In fact it is rubbish. If this is how you find yourself then all I can say is I know how hard that is, but it should get better.

Social media is not for everyone. I didn't used to think it would be for me, but I was wrong. For those of us who use it, it can offer a great deal of friendship and support. When I first started using Twitter there were a handful of other adopters using it. Now there are lots and we enjoy a space where we can be funny, honest, sad, angry, happy, frustrated and supportive. If you think it might offer you something then give it a try.

Leaving the house

Leaving the house can be a scary thing to do, especially for new adopters. The house offers a certain degree of containment and predictability which is not the case in the street, at the supermarket or in someone else's house. Our own homes and lives have been adjusted to suit our child, fine-tuned for maximum safety (and I'm not just talking about cupboard locks here). It is right that our child feels entirely accepted and loved at home, but what about when we go out? What can we do to make sure that children are kept safe and feel a sense of belonging?

How Mr D. and I have raised our children without them being knocked over by a car or drowned I really don't know. They had no sense of danger at all. Walking two small children to playgroup or school when both want to run off and pick something interesting up from the middle of the road is no mean feat. Going swimming was even worse. The youngest and most likely to drown would run out of the changing room (to the sound of me shouting 'WALK!'), through the showers, perhaps slip over on the way, perhaps not, and then perform a running jump into the swimming pool. She was a toddler. If you ever want to feel the full sting of other people's disapproval, it's a good way to go about it.

Attracting disapproval is par for the course as an adoptive parent. Our children were such danger-monkeys I had to buy reins and use the pushchair as a means of keeping control. People don't like out-of-control children and they disapprove of mothers who use reins. I came not to care. The reins were the only thing stopping our angelic daughter from throwing herself in front of a truck, or holding out her hand to touch a snarling dog. We graduated from reins and from the accusing looks of others after a long process of 'You must walk sensibly here, or hold my hand, which do you choose?' I often had to take a writhing hand in mine and take control. Sometimes safety has to come first. No, there's no 'I wonder why you find it hard to hold my hand' when we're out and there are trucks.

For our eldest child as a young teenager, the world outside our front door is populated by risky people and dangerous situations. Walking down the street of our small town isn't any longer about running about and being out of control but about having the senses bombarded. He finds it hard to assess what isn't a risk and what is, to navigate his way around pushchairs, wheelchairs, slow pedestrians and fast pedestrians. He will be distracted by a person who he considers to look 'dodgy', or by a builder drilling a bit of pavement, or a police officer. We are increasingly having to practise walking along a section of street without bumping into anyone. We set manageable tasks and they have to be carried out with understanding. None of that, 'For goodness sake look where you're going' is going to improve things. Being 'hyper-alert' and in a situation where there are lots of things to be alert about is like a double-whammy.

I don't want to come over too negatively and so now I shall ask permission to boast a bit. I only tell you this because you may be finding it hard to imagine ever leaving the house without having your adrenal glands whipped into a state of exhaustion. We have always been able to go out for a meal as a family. No one runs around. No one shouts. No one is silly. And Mr D. and I have twice been complemented by restaurant owners about how marvellously well-behaved our children are. We could of course be unusual, but I have talked to other adopters who have the same dining out experiences. By the way, I find the whole complementing parents on the behaviour of their children thing quite vomit-inducing, but there you go. When I really try to analyse why our children cope well when we go out for a meal, I think there are a few factors. First, for us, going out in public and respecting other people is a stake in the ground. If we couldn't eat out without pissing other people off, then we wouldn't go. Second, I think they enjoy going out to eat and they like it when Mr D. and I enjoy ourselves too. It's a low-stress treat and they don't want to mess up.

Learning about the situations our children can cope with easily, cope with given support and can't cope with at all is a long process and things change over time. We once had a family day out in London. It was horrendous. It blew our son's mind and we should never have taken him. I think we were still in the final flushes of delusion that our lives could and should be like everyone else's (and everyone else can take their family to London for the day, right?). Now I've realised that it's all right to push at the boundaries a bit, occasionally and carefully. And we give the choice 'do you fancy going to x for the day this weekend, or do you think it will be too much?' If we go to x and it becomes distressing, then we take time out and sit in the park or cut the day short. We always make sure we give ourselves plenty of flexibility. Many of us kick against this amount of planning and improvising (I did), but it is the way things have to be.

Children making friends

'I haven't got any friends.'

'I sat by myself at lunchtime because no one wanted to play with me.'

'I was the only one who didn't get an invitation to the party.'

Isn't it shitty to hear your child say these things? Having friends is a validation that we are likeable individuals. Not having friends must be one of the worst feelings in the world.

There are no two ways about it, children with broken attachments and crushing low self-esteem find the business of forming friendships baffling. Watching them try to fail is heart-breaking.

There are three things at play here. The first and most significant is that our children don't understand all the rules of friendship and so don't get how they work. Friendships are complicated things, even for the most healthily attached amongst us. Second, our children, being in some respects developmentally younger than their peers, can present as being a bit immature or a bit silly. Third, some mean and stupid parents dissuade their children from being friends with ours because they have 'come from the care system' and are therefore tainted somehow. Shame on them.

I'll start with a word on mean and stupid parents. Here is a blog post I wrote a couple of years ago. I published it anonymously but now feel brave enough to stand by it. It is raw and jagged so perhaps skip it if you aren't in the right place for raw and jagged.

My daughter, adopted and traumatised, but nevertheless happy, fun, sociable and kind, until last year went to a small, cosy village primary with a 'family feel'.

She had been best friends from the start with a little girl who I'll call Ruby. They sat together, played together, ate lunch together. Great.

Then two years ago Ruby publicly handed out invitations to her birthday party. She gave them to all the girls in the class, with one exception, my daughter. My daughter was puzzled and kept saying, 'I'm sure I'll get one soon, she accidently left mine at home' and then 'Ruby said she ran out of pens to write my invitation and her mum has to buy some more.' She was sad, stung and full of shame. She thought it was her fault. I was f**king livid.

We survived the episode and a few months later Ruby approached me in the playground and asked if she could come to our house to play after school. I swallowed down bile, approached the mother and it was arranged. 'You'll have to come to our house next,' the mother bleated as my daughter's face lit up. No invitation ever materialised.

Fast forward another year, another birthday party and another repeat performance. Again, every other girl in the class was invited, even casual acquaintances. My daughter was left feeling bereft.

A few weeks later and a year ago now the daughter who never cries found a tear rolling down her cheek. I suggested we think about moving to a larger, local middle school, where there would be a greater choice of friends. She beamed, then jumped up and down with excitement and hasn't looked back since.

Ruby's parents are both involved in charity work – loudly and publicly. They are the sort of people who say 'bless' a lot. They are full of crap. Recently she tried to 'friend' me on Facebook. If there had been a 'f**k off and die' button I'd have used it. Ruby rings our number regularly and leaves many, many messages. Can I come to your house? Can I come today? Tomorrow? My daughter is so forgiving that she looks at me with unbearable hope in her eyes.

Over my dead body.

These are the sort of people who think that 'delinquent' children should be locked up in borstals and drugged. Yes, that was one pleasant playground conversation. Charitable, my arse. I have no doubt that they judged my daughter to be a bad influence, someone who, because of her beginnings, wasn't going to turn out well. The multiple acts of casual cruelty they inflicted caused terrible upset to someone who did nothing to deserve it. But do you know what? Their lives are all the poorer for it.

The good news is that our daughter moved to a large middle school near to where we live, which, on the face of it, might not have suited her as well as the small and 'family-orientated' village primary she was going to, but she hasn't looked back. Part of the reason is that there is a much wider choice of children to be friends with and her eccentricities are accepted and valued. I learnt that we can't force friendships to happen, but we can do something about the environment.

Before our children started school I had heard from other adoptive parents that their children tended to gravitate towards 'the least suitable children'. I thought it all sounded a bit like middle-class worry-mongery and rather spurious until our elder child, at the age of five, teamed up with the children of the local criminals. I tried my best to be all open-minded and accepting until he started coming out with things he'd heard at school which made my hair stand on end. I can't say what they were, but if true, involved some serious child protection issues. I found out that the families concerned were not unfamiliar with social services and the police, and not for good reasons. I tried to explain to my son why he might want to make some other friends, if only to balance things out a bit. It made no difference, it was as though he was magnetically attracted to them. Before I knew it he was wanting to go to their houses for sleepovers. And then he was being threatened. Other children didn't want to associate with him because he was 'one of the naughty ones'. I knew enough to realise that being branded as 'one of the naughty ones' was a very bad thing. Then I was being approached in the playground by scary dads asking about play dates. Shit, I thought, how did that happen?

The school said that there was little they could do to help our son out of the frightening place in which he found himself. As far as they were concerned he was choosing his friends and had to learn about friendships the hard way. I could see that he was vulnerable and lost and was going to school and making terrible choices without the ability to do otherwise and without understanding the consequences. There are lots of theories about why our children seem to have to play out their worst nightmares and some of them are not very nice to think about. The important question is, do we let this kind of scenario play itself out, or do we intervene?

I thought about my role as parent/scaffolder and chose to intervene. Eventually, after trying really hard to help him to make the right choices, I realised that we were on to a loser. Other factors came into play and we moved school. There were no children at the new school that I wouldn't have wanted him to be friends with. He made friends and he made mistakes, but he made both in a safe environment.

It is really important, I've found, to use lots of empathy when mistakes are made. There will be times when our children are tempted by another child who is doing something risky and exciting and they get upset or get into trouble as a consequence. With our help they gradually learn the consequences resulting from different choices. One day you will hear them say, 'I don't feel good when I hang around with x, I think you were right about them' and you will feel tempted to punch the air and say, 'I told you so', but you won't will you? Promise?

We are taught not to judge a book by its cover, but in reality we make judgements about people all the time. Occasionally we get it wrong and adjust our thinking. It's important that we learn these skills because not everyone is safe or helpful to be around. If someone stands in the street swearing loudly and intimidating passersby with a dog, then I think we are wise to give them a wide berth. Making judgements to keep ourselves safe is not the same as being judgemental. Sometimes it *is* best to judge a book by its cover.

As with so much of adoptive parenting, it is important to keep the faith. Our children often lag behind their peers in lots of ways and particularly in matters of friendship, but they get there eventually. Both of our children started to 'get' friendships and experience success just as I was starting to give up hope. Attachment experts say that children need to experience and feel secure in their relationships with their nearest and dearest before they feel safe enough to venture out and start to form attachments in the wider world. This rings true in our family. Sometimes I think about those films where a toddler in a coffee shop will wander away from its mother to explore the space around it, and return back to her every few minutes, just to check that she is still there and it's safe to venture out again. It feels like my children do this, even now.

Gaining independence

In some ways childhood is one long preparation for independence, and independence is like a house: if the foundations are flimsy, the whole thing will come tumbling down.

If I plotted our children's progress along Independence Street it would not come out as a straight line, but would look more like the stock market: very up and down with some good times and some crashes, but broadly displaying growth. It is sometimes difficult to see progress when in the middle of an economic downturn, but it comes in its own good time.

Waving your child off to the park on their own for the very first time can be daunting, but sooner or later, when the time is right, it has to be done. It is difficult to say for sure when the time is right. It is much easier to say when the time is wrong. The time is wrong when our child is going through a difficult patch and making unwise choices. The time is wrong when they are angry and hate us. The time is wrong when you think it is likely that they will fail.

I have taken a lengthening rope approach to independence. I let out a little at a time and pull it back in if the resulting freedom has been too much for my child to cope with. It started with short amounts of time close to home, some of which were monitored from a distance. We've now graduated to trips into town with friends on the bus. I still say 'no' if we are in the middle of an economic downturn. My strong suspicion is that if things are being broken and I'm being sworn at, the ground isn't at that time fertile enough in which to grow independence. I have been known to say, in advance of a planned excursion:

> 'I know that you want to go out at the weekend, so I need to let you know now that if your emotions continue to be strong and a bit out of control then you'll need to stay close to home.'

That is so much more palatable and less inflammatory than, 'If you don't calm down and stop throwing shoes at me then you're not going out this weekend.'

He might not always admit it, but our son knows that we are doing our best to help keep him safe.

Breaking away

I well remember as a teenager sometimes feeling as though I could quite happily murder someone, so strong were my feelings. I was lucky that friends provided me with an outlet and plenty of opportunities to spend time away from home. I grew up in a good and happy family, but nevertheless, the teenage years were hard at times. I try to remember these feelings as I now find myself the parent of a teenage son and soon-to-be teenage daughter.

There were times when I could quite happily have run for it. I think that's quite natural. Instead I stomped around our local recreation ground wondering why my life was so terrible (it wasn't) and dreaming of meeting a handsome yet troubled boy walking an adorable dog golden retriever (it never happened, although I did meet some not very handsome boys in that park but that's a whole other story).

The fact is, getting some space around us is sometimes the best way of letting off steam which might otherwise prove to be destructive. I've found it best to explore feelings like this and practical ways of coping when times are calm.

> 'I understand what it's like when you literally want to explode. If you need to, it's alright to go out for a walk or a cycle.'

You can tell them funny stories about how you felt and behaved as a teenager. Mine always find stories of my misdemeanours hysterically funny and they can start to understand me as a fallible person rather than an all-knowing, all-controlling parent(!).

I am no expert in raising teenagers, and I know that some adoptive families experience the very worst of times during the teenage years. It's when the really scary stuff comes into sight: smoking, drinking, drugs, sex, self-harming. It's when as parents we start to realise that we can't change the world and that sometimes trauma runs so deep that the measures of success change. I know of some heartbreaking situations, which I would change in a heartbeat if I could. Some of them could, I suspect, have been avoided with the right therapeutic support from the start. Others may have been inevitable no matter what support was available.

Sometimes the urge to run is about big, frightening feelings and a mother who won't stop nagging and a dad who just doesn't understand and a teacher who expects too much. We have to try our hardest to allow our children to experience these feelings and to accept them.

As our children grow up we have to adjust our hard-learnt parenting styles. They are going to use bad language, try out things we'd rather they didn't, hang about wearing clothes we don't like, flicking hair we don't like. That's not to say that all the boundaries fade away because they don't, but to some extent success through these teenage years depends on keeping relationships going and channels of communication open, and for that we need to remember what it was like to be a teenager.

We do a lot of 'What would happen if' scenarios in our house and this is as much about listening as they are talking. Giving a teenager the opportunity to explain to you what enrages their rages and what calms them is effective in itself. I've been told some home truths which I've had to accept with grace. Much of this is about our children being helped to recognise their feelings and where they might lead to and to take alternative action. Eventually we hope to get to a place where a child can say, 'I'm feeling really angry and I might burst so keep away from me, I need to go to my room.' I've been able to explain what would happen if either of our children really, properly, ran away (rather than pretend run away). We've been through how I would have to call the police and social services, and what might then happen as a result. I don't do this to scare them, but just to explore it a little. I believe that doing this takes away some of the threat and some of the excitement. It is also helping to build narrative and consequential thinking. If a child can stop for just a moment to think, 'Hang on, if I carry on like this…' then a crisis may be averted.

CHAPTER 9

'LIFE STORY WORK'

Not only does Life Story Work have a terrible title, it is one of the most difficult and most contentious areas adoptive families have to face.

Whoever was in charge of the branding exercise and decided that connecting the words 'life' with 'work' and 'story' should be fired. But unfortunately the term has stuck, and so reluctantly I'll use it.

For those of us fortunate enough to have been gifted happy, healthy childhoods, our lives are one lovely whole which our memories and thoughts are free to travel around without fear. For our children, however, the past is fractured, confusing and frightening and its pieces have been locked away in a box, wrapped in fear and shame, and secured with a ribbon of low self-esteem. Going near the box, let alone attempting to open it, takes bravery and confidence on all sides.

I can't give advice about how to approach Life Story Work because I am nowhere near experienced or qualified enough. I can only describe how we've gone about it, which is not always how we've been told to go about it. Being blunt, Life Story Work has been the biggest source of disconnect between the advice we've been given and the tangled, red raw reality.

Much of the advice I've had is that Life Story Work is something to be scheduled, organised and tidied, and which must be started almost immediately your child is placed with you. You might prepare a table with a Life Story Book on it (a dog-eared ring binder with a motley collection of photographs), some lovely big sheets of clean, white paper, some new pens and you might say, 'We're going to do some Life Story Work now' as though imposing neatness is somehow going to make what's inside the box any more likely to come out or any more bearable.

My own overwhelming experience is that Life Story Work is messy, confusing, organic, dynamic, disorganised, repetitive and unpredictable. More than that, it is so much part of family life it cannot be unravelled from the whole. It certainly can't be scheduled.

I received a lot of criticism, when I really didn't need it, for not doing some kind of formal life story torture with our children when they were very young (in fact I once went on a course where *I* was used as the 'how not to do it' case study). It was thought that I was trying to erase the past, trying to forget it ever existed, reinforce my dominance as parent-present, or that I was simply too scared to go there. It was none of the above. Every time I tried to get near the box, our children became highly and disturbingly distressed. They also, in my opinion, were too young at the time to understand even basic family relationships let alone the sprawling mess that is their birth family. It seemed like they needed a break from the red raw difficult things. They needed time to heal and time to attach to us. I took their lead and I took the criticism too.

Since concluding for myself that our children needed a slower, more thoughtful and yet more dynamic approach to Life Story Work than that I was being encouraged to carry out, I've begun talking to adoptees about their experiences of coming to terms with a fractured and traumatic past. One wrote:

> *Having a bad past is like having a Pandora's box inside of you. Pulling it open, as I might imagine a psychiatrist would want to do, can be immensely destructive. It's only worth letting out what you can process – and if you have no mechanism in place to do that you're in trouble. Some people seem to think talking through it resolves it – well, abuses that run deep need to be*

physically resolved in my experience. Clearing up the conscious mind's relationship to it is literally the tip of the iceberg.

Another, Fran, told me:

Contrary to what you might for a time believe, or are taught to believe, what happens to you isn't something you can or should just go back to, open a page to, sit in a room for an hour, discuss and are able to just get over or automatically understand. It's the effects of what's happened that seep into your everyday life that you have to live with. However, if you can learn to recognise some of these and manage them differently – the less of a hold the cause has over you and the stronger you will become.

Physically working through trauma is something which I am only just starting to understand the significance of. Calming the mind and the body either through doing activities outdoors, or drawing, cooking or clay modelling or whatever, are things that I know are beneficial to our children. Fran and another adoptee have also told me that for them, frequently returning to, or being made to return to, the past has been of little use to them. What has been important has been building a strong, resilient foundation for life and for the future, partly by developing and practising coping mechanisms. From this stronger base, the past can be carefully explored, and life's fast balls can be faced without danger of bringing the house down. I am very grateful for the honesty and generosity of both Fran and the other adoptee who have shared their experiences with me.

After I called a halt to the Life Story torture, our children's Life Story Books were put on a shelf, accessible, but not where they would be seen many times a day. We got on with life in the present, growing closer to each other, establishing routines and traditions and taking on new challenges like starting pre-school and school. The books did not get touched or referred to for the next two years. That's not to say that we side-stepped adoption as a subject area when it came up naturally. We talked about it in short bursts and in a straightforward and natural way.

Gradually questions started to come to which I gave honest answers, appropriate to what I thought our children were ready and able to understand and process (perhaps they felt ready to open Pandora's box a little). Each time we talked I gave a bit more, growing their knowledge and stretching their tiny little zones of comfort. If they asked for more information, I gave it and sometimes a bit more. Over time the questions became more frequent and more often than not came when we were in the car. A great deal of our Life Story Work has been done in the car, parked outside school. There are reasons why our children choose to ask for the answers to life's most painful questions in the car and I think we should respect that. The car gives physical and psychological distance. It means that you, as the driver, cannot walk off and do something else, neither can you initiate painful and uncomfortable eye-contact, and it means that the conversation has a cut-off time, whether that's the end of the journey or the school bell. I often suggested that we delay going into school if they needed some thinking time, but they only did that once. I think they wanted to be able to run into school and press the 'pause' button on the pain of the past. Once we got back home at the end of the day I would always refer back to our earlier conversation and let them know we could continue to talk, or not. Sometimes the questions would start again and sometimes they wouldn't.

By the age of ten, our son had seen and read all the information about his past that we have at home. He now uses song lyrics (particularly those by Professor Green and Eminem), drawings, diagrams and startlingly honest pieces of writing to express how he feels about his life so far. I am lucky that he has taken the lead and I'm glad that I put him in the driving seat. He has shown remarkable insight, honesty and bravery throughout the process.

Our daughter is travelling at her own pace, asking her own questions, and I am equally confident that she will arrive at a healthy understanding of her life. She sometimes shows more shame around what happened to her in the past, and I might have to lead a bit more strongly, but I know when to step forward and when to back off.

It is during Life Story Work that the brittle voice is shouting to be heard and when we must be most aware of listening to it and not denying its truths. 'I must have been a bad baby' is a terrible thing to hear a child say, and we must brace against the desire to wrestle this from them using the full force of denial. 'Do you think you were a bad baby?' is a more fruitful, but more painful path to take and then, 'It must be truly awful to feel you were a bad baby.' It is helpful to look at pictures of babies or to think about babies you know and to ask whether they are bad babies. The answer will most probably be 'no', which sets up a fracture between this discovery and how our child thinks of their tiny selves. They may try to paper over the fracture with, 'But I was a bad baby.' The inference is that they deserved all that happened to them, because what other reason could there be for a parent to neglect, abuse or reject their child? These sorts of conversations may open up deep wells of anger or sadness, or a mixture of both. Whichever it is, we have to be strong enough to hold them and let ourselves feel a little of it too. I have often cried with them and raged with them, which demonstrates that their feelings are valid and acceptable and they are safe to share them.

'What happened to you was wrong' is a phrase I've used as well as, 'I wish I could have been there to take care of you.' The hardest part I've found is to try to help them to explore the grey areas that mark the unmapped marshes between right and wrong. One of our children is very clear that there were no possible excuses for what happened to him, and I respect that. Our other child is taking the first steps into exploring whether her birth parent had the skills and experience to raise her as she deserved to be raised. It's a lot more difficult than it's often made out to be.

Most adopted children own a collection of photographs of birth family members. Our experience of having and looking at these pictures has not exactly followed the textbooks either. There are several pictures which I am certain re-traumatises one of our children, and I don't know whether their power will ever be extinguished. An educational psychologist we worked with for a short time (who was made redundant soon after completing some great work for us) once asked me a question which stopped me in my tracks: if you had been kidnapped and violently attacked by a man, would you choose to keep looking at a photograph of him? Of course the answer was, 'No, I wouldn't.' It made me think differently about the 'Let's sit and look through your Life Story Book' scenario. It's important to remember that some of the photographs belonging to our children will hold extraordinary power. It's another reason why I prefer to give our children a degree of control. Our children are the real life history experts, not us, and so we must stand by them, bear witness to their feelings and reactions and learn from them. That's my experience anyway.

However you decide to approach the vast subject of Life Story Work, I wish you bravery and fortitude. It drags us to the depths and the heights of human possibility, and for that reason it is important to make sure we have good emotional support around us. Our children need us to be a reliable and strong place of safety and good sense from which they can start to explore some frightening places.

It is of course tempting to paper over the past, to just not go there and to fix our eyes firmly and optimistically on the future. The battle with past trauma isn't one that optimism can ever hope to win. My experience is that, despite needing to exercise care over when and how much Pandora's box is opened, it can't be locked shut and hidden in an empty room. In fact, the more we try to forget about it, the greater the chance the contents will burst out uncontrollably and destructively. If you are in any doubt about the need to venture near the box at all, then here is something our son wrote a few months ago, without any prompting from me. It was addressed to a parent whose son was experiencing extreme anger outbursts:

> When you get the chance and he is nice and calm just sit him down gradually tell him about his past or why he was removed from his 'birth family.' Because that has helped me; he will be shocked at first and it will take time to sink in, but it will work 99.9 per cent.

CHAPTER 10

SELF-CARE

Relax. This chapter is all about you and is a little easier going, mostly.

First, I'm going to stick my neck out and tell you something which I have learnt to be a fundamental truth about being a therapeutic parent and which no one has ever told me. THE MOST IMPORTANT PART OF BEING AN EFFECTIVE THERAPEUTIC PARENT IS SELF-CARE. I wish someone had let me into that secret a long time ago.

Many of us don't feel comfortable caring for ourselves. Putting one's own wellbeing first is considered to be kind of rude and selfish. Far better and more 'polite' to be a martyr. Adoptive parenting is no game for martyrs. It will eat martyrs alive (slowly and painfully).

We are the column that holds up the building, the dam which holds back the flood, the life raft which others cling to. If we give way, everything is lost. It is therefore crucial that we do not give way. Just remember what we're told on airplanes: put on your own oxygen mask before you attempt to fit your child's. It's very good advice.

The term 'take care of the carers' is a blindingly obvious piece of socio-economic bullshit. It ought to be practised, but it isn't. There is little care for the carers and so we must do most of it for ourselves. This may make you want to drop to the floor and cry into the onion skins of life again, but actually, once you've got your head around self-care, it's liberating. And sometimes you can use it to get out of things you don't want to do (but don't tell anyone I told you that).

Secondary trauma

I'm going to darken the tone a little here and tell you about what can happen if you do not take care of yourself. It happened to me. It happened to me because our son was super-traumatised, I was still learning how to be a decent therapeutic parent and I was doing too much.

I didn't used to know this (I should have done) but trauma is catching. You can get it from spending a long time with someone else who has it. Trauma is in the air and it catches in the hair, is breathed into the lungs and clings to the skin. It invades the brain and hijacks the emotions. It feels like something has stolen your identity, like a horrible alien parasite. Mr D. and I were both struck down by it, at the same time. It was the worst experience of my life. I became hyper-sensitive to noise (worried that a sound meant a fight was about to start, or something was being smashed), I was constantly braced for action and pumped full of adrenaline, I couldn't settle to anything, even to read a book, I felt scared for the future and I carried a deep sense of hopelessness (nothing I do will make any difference), and I felt overwhelmed. After a particularly bad weekend I felt myself shutting down. I didn't have an ounce of spare energy and I ceased to feel any emotion. I wandered around the house like a disaster victim. I was empty. Sometimes I cried for long periods of time and then I went back to empty again.

Luckily at this time some close family members stepped in and looked after our children for a week. It saved us. Mr D. and I spent that week in numb, white shock. We didn't know what to do with ourselves. We thought we ought to make the most of having some time together, but we had zero energy. We mostly ate toast and laid around staring into space.

If it hadn't been for our social worker we may never have accepted that offer of respite from our family members. She swiped away all the doubts and the 'yes but's' and helped us to see the bigger picture of the dam holding back the million gallons of water. Self-care is now part of the fabric of our family lives and we practise it without guilt.

I feel duty bound to point out here that if you really find yourself in a relentless, deep, dark place, which you can't see a way out of, then it is advisable to seek medical advice. I didn't because I knew why I was feeling bleak and because I worry that secondary trauma gets confused with depression. But if you are in any doubt, then please go and visit your GP.

Living the dream

Modern life as fed to us through television programmes, magazines and advertising is demanding of parents and especially demanding of mothers. Its messages seep into our brains and multiply and invade us.

Thou shalt keep a clean, boutique-hotel style home, maintain germ-free surfaces babies could eat their dinner off, cook locally-sourced, seasonal ingredients from scratch, grow your own vegetables, eat five of them a day (preferably seven), do yoga, practise mindfulness, keep chickens, have fragrant children who play instruments which come in large cases, take said children on educational trips to museums, read improving books to them, enforce strict screen time limits, recycle plastics, up cycle cardboard, put out bird food all year (not just in winter), maintain a healthy BMI, glowing skin and a positive 'can do' attitude.

Enough!

Success as a therapeutic parent means waving goodbye to the super-clean-efficient-robo-alpha-parent-slave. It's time to focus on what's important. After my unpleasant sojourn into secondary trauma my objective changed from 'be mildly marvellous in most areas' to 'keep family together'. I've now adjusted upwards to 'raise happy children whilst remaining sane'.

Taking a Me Holiday

If you find yourself heading towards a dark place, then you might benefit from taking a 'Me Holiday'. You won't find a Me Holiday in the brochures. It isn't (unfortunately) two weeks in an all-inclusive beachside villa having your every need catered for whilst sipping cocktails and eating Lindt chocolate. But it is the only way I know of getting back on our feet whilst maintaining 'good enough' parenting. This isn't parenting with any frills whatsoever; it is budget supermarket rather than delicatessen. It is functional. It is 'everyone is wearing something and no one smells of wee' rather than 'everyone looks gorgeous and has completed 30 minutes of harp practice'.

This is my Me Holiday Guide. My Me Holiday lasts as long as I need it to. I might book it in advance or I might take it at a moment's notice. It all depends. You are most welcome to use my Holiday Guide, or you could develop your own.

Fast food

Go shopping somewhere quiet and non-taxing (or go online) and buy food which doesn't need much preparation. Beans on toast, baked potatoes, prepared salads, fruit and yoghurts are all healthy and fuss-free. No one is going to starve or develop scurvy from eating these for a couple of weeks. Chuck in some pizzas and some ready meals and something from the takeaway and you will find the catering weight is lifted. This is a good thing if you are running on empty. Hours a week will be released for quality recuperation (vegging) time.

A fall in standards

Drop standards of tidiness and cleanliness. Think, 'What's the worst that could happen if I don't vacuum this hall carpet right now?' If the answer is, 'It'll be on my mind' then for goodness sake, get a grip. This is a Me Holiday. Get lazy. Get slovenly.

Me time

Get some time on your own, perhaps when the children are at school or playgroup, or ask someone to look after them for you and plan to do exactly what you feel like doing. Watch trashy television (although see point 4 below), listen to music, eat crisps. Do it without guilt. Do it for as many days as you need to. If you feel a great exhaustion washing over, that's because you are tired out and you need a rest, maybe even lots of sleep.

A happy place

Nurture happiness.

Avoid doing things which make you feel worse rather than better for doing them. Do not watch any television which (a) contains shouting; (b) is sad; (c) involves a studio audience; (d) sets ridiculously high domestic standards. My own happy place excludes *The Jeremy Kyle Show*, *Brokeback Mountain*, *Question Time* and anything involving icing bags.

Stay away from Drains. Did you know there are only two types of people: Drains and Radiators? Radiators are people who make you feel better just by being in their presence. Drains are the opposite (you know the ones, always moaning on about something). You can't afford to lose any more of your precious energy to a Drain.

Listen to music which makes you want to dance in the kitchen. Dance in the kitchen.

Watch funny YouTube clips of people falling over and Fern Britton making innuendoes.

Rediscover the bin

The bin is the big, plastic thing in the corner of the kitchen (or if you are posh, the shiny, silver thing in the corner of the kitchen). Whilst you are on your Me Holiday, put all rubbish in this receptacle. Do not separate out plastics, wash out sardine tins, carry leaking bags of rotten carrot peelings down the garden in your slippers. Not very green, I know, but this is a temporary state of affairs whilst you get back on your feet. And don't forget, the worst thing for the planet is human procreation, so with all you've done to limit population growth, you have the carbon footprint of a dormouse. Now stand back and see how much tidier your house looks.

Say 'no'

Cut out all volunteering. Do not bake cakes, do not man stalls, do not go on school trips, do not take meeting minutes. Remember, this is a Me Holiday. Practise using the word 'no' with meaning.

'Would you like to jump backwards to Carlisle for a good cause?'

'No.'

'Would you like to be a school governor? We're really short of volunteers.'

'No.'

'Could you come on the school trip because we are short of adults and if you don't come the children won't be able to go?'

'No.'

It might not be very Big Society, but as an adopter you are the embodiment of the Big Society. Society benefits from the job you are doing (though admittedly it isn't always very good at showing its appreciation), and that gives you a 'Get Out of the PTA Free' card. Use it.

If you are still wavering and coming over guilt-stricken and all 'the school/church hall committee will collapse without me', just imagine Sir Bradley Wiggins is approached in the playground of his children's school by the head of the PTA.

> Head of PTA: 'Sir Bradley, I wonder if you'd be able to bake a cake for the sports day cake stall, a Victoria sponge perhaps?'
>
> Sir Bradley: 'No, I'm far too busy with my cycling, sorry.'
>
> Head of PTA (disappointed and pained face): 'Oh that's a shame. Well, maybe you could sell raffle tickets then?'
>
> Sir Bradley: 'Nope. Too busy.'
>
> Head of PTA (transmitting powerful guilt pangs): 'Ahhh, that's a shame…'
>
> Sir Bradley: 'Must be off. Another 50 to do before lunch, then it's on to the treadmill.'

Why doesn't Sir Bradley bake cakes for sports day? Sell a few raffle tickets? Read with the year 1s? Because he's a VERY BUSY MAN. And what are you doing that is so much more important than cycling? NURTURING TRAUMATISED CHILDREN. The reason why Sir Bradley is immune to the head of the PTA is that he is certain that what he is doing is more important and he is focused on his priorities (plus he's a man). Get focused.

Raising and healing traumatised children is like cycling a stage of the Tour de France. Every day. When someone is throwing upholstery tacks at you.

Saying 'yes'

That relative who keeps offering to look after the children? The student who is available for babysitting duties? The friend who could easily pick your child up from school and give them tea? Say 'yes' to them all, right away. Don't listen to your inner uber-mother who tells you, 'It will unsettle the children, don't do it.' It will unsettle them a whole lot more if you have a breakdown. And all good holiday resorts have a kids' club, right?

If no one has offered any help, then go out and ask for it. Approach family members and friends and tell them you are struggling and need some help. Most people are happy to assist and are just waiting to be asked. If you have a partner, don't forget to share with them how you feel. Don't wait until you can no longer get out of bed in the morning.

If you have a partner, go out with them. Remember what it is you love about each other. Talk without being interrupted. Feel what it's like to laugh without having a sweaty hand clamped over your mouth.

Call on the flat screen babysitter

You've holidayed a little and now the children are back home. They want to make salt dough dinosaurs. They want to go to the fun session at the swimming pool. They want to learn how to crochet. These activities are for another day. For now, put on a film, lie on the sofa with them for an hour or two or more and vegetate until it's time to switch on the microwave. As well as being a 'low impact' activity it also counts as close supervision (see Chapter 11, Practical Techniques) which is good for our children.

Suspend homework

It is perfectly acceptable, and desirable, that during a Me Holiday homework is suspended. I find a quick telephone call to school, something like, 'I'm terribly sorry but we are currently experiencing a small family crisis and we won't be able to complete any homework for the next week' works well.

Treat night

Once the children are in bed (early nights are permissible, particularly if they can't tell the time) bring out the treats. Nice chocolates, posh crisps, humus, wine, whatever floats your (life) boat. A Me Holiday is not the time for a diet. It is about feeding the soul and putting yourself back on your feet again.

A longer-term strategy

It is better for everybody that we don't get so ground down by life that we need to take an extended Me Holiday. Supporting adopted children requires extra parenting for a very long time, and the energy and resilience to do this has to come from somewhere. For many of us it means making permanent or at least semi-permanent adjustments to life. Here are some of the adjustments I've had to make.

Mental adjustment

Children who have experienced traumatic times, as we know, do not just 'get over it'. Better to come to terms with this than to live in hope that one day all will be fixed. This process took me a long time and was painful, but once I'd accepted reality for what it was, it allowed me to square up to it and get tooled up for the job.

Be kind to yourself

Continue to take guilt-free time for yourself and enjoy it.

Be kind to each other

If you are parenting your children with a partner, look out for each other and give each other a break now and again and do something nice for each other. Make time away from the children to gather strength and find the love. You need to be a strong team. Trauma is no respecter of long-term relationships, in fact, it is threatened by them.

Get educated

Go on all the courses you can and become an expert in therapeutic parenting. There is always something to learn and something to be reminded of. This will not only build your skills and knowledge, but your confidence too. Confidence is like rocket fuel in this game. If you are parenting with a partner, then make sure BOTH of you get educated. Therapeutic parenting isn't something which can be allocated to one person, like putting the bins out.

Find support

Find a support network either locally, further afield or through social media, which works for you. Make sure it is genuinely supportive and not just a group of people indulging in competitive whinging. It should make you feel better, not worse, for going, lighter, not heavier, and understood rather than misunderstood.

Forgive yourself

We all make mistakes and react in untherapeutic ways from time to time. Forgive. Learn. Move on. It's part of being human.

Don't take on too much

You never know what is around the corner so think carefully before committing your time. If your one night out a month is

to a school governors' meeting, then be honest about whether
you'd rather be spending that evening in the pub or at the
cinema instead.

Embrace labour-saving devices
Buying a dishwasher saved my sanity and quite possibly my
marriage. Buying an in-car DVD player did the same.

Celebrate successes
Success in our families might not look the same as success in
other people's families. Success might be our child going on
a school trip, or entering a competition, or icing a digestive
biscuit, but it is no less significant for that. Stop now and again
to reflect on how far you've all come. Appreciate the view.

Have fun
Fun isn't necessarily going to London to visit the Natural History
Museum, or spending a weekend in a theme park (both would
be the polar opposite of fun in our family). Fun can be going out
for fish and chips or sharing a bowl of sweets or throwing stones
into a river. Find the joy.

CHAPTER 11

PRACTICAL TECHNIQUES

Better to go and watch a man digging, and then take a spade and try to do it, and go on trying till it comes, and you gain the knack that is to be learnt with all tools, of doubling the power and halving the effort; and meanwhile you will be learning other things, about your own arms and legs and back, and perhaps a little robin will come and give you moral support, and at the same time keep a sharp look-out for any worms you may happen to turn up.

Gertrude Jekyll

My toolbox is pretty well-stocked now, with useful bits and pieces which I've borrowed from various books, professionals and other adopters I've come across along the way, and techniques I've developed myself. The techniques I've developed myself have come about sometimes through gut instinct, sometimes by accident and sometimes through careful thought because nothing else I had was up to the job. This has happened much more often as our children have got older and some of the trusty older tools have worn out. As the great artist and gardener Gertrude Jekyll says, the best tools make lighter work of a heavy job. Using them to their full potential takes practice, and in the practice we learn things about ourselves which we'd never have learnt otherwise. Here is a selection of those techniques which have worked particularly well in our family, some of which I've alluded to elsewhere. I invite you to borrow any that look like they might be useful. I'm sure that you have your own too.

Close supervision

Close supervision is my go to technique when things are spiralling out of control. I stick with our children from the moment they get home from school, until they go to bed. It's a quick cheese on toast for tea, watching films together and 'think toddler' in action. It creates feelings of safety, lowers anxiety and reduces the chances they have to fail. It needs a good couple of weeks to start working and probably longer. Once you start to see real improvement, continue on until the changes are embedded (I have pulled back too early in the past and regretted it). Reduce the close supervision gradually and if things start to deteriorate, ramp it up again. I can't pretend it's easy to do, but it can calm an angry and chaotic household. The reduction in challenging behaviours will more than make up for the effort. Reduce domestic chores to a bare minimum whilst you are practising close supervision. It's advisable not to tell your children you are embarking on it, or to present it as a punishment. Ours enjoy close supervision or 'Mum time'.

Emergency plan

When our family was being buffeted by extreme anger and violence I talked to our neighbours, both police officers, about what life was like for us, and asked them if I could call on them if I was ever in a situation that was getting out of hand. I am grateful to them for agreeing to be part of my emergency plan and for not finding my request at all bizarre or inappropriate. Just having them close by and knowing that I can call on them has helped a great deal. I don't know what the future will hold, whether the improving times will continue, or whether we have more troubling times ahead, but either way I mean to check in with my neighbours every once in a while, just to make sure my plan is still in place.

Random acts of kindness

'I was thinking of you today and so I bought you this comic' demonstrates to your child that you are bound up with them and hold them with you at all times. It contradicts their fear that they are forgotten and alone when you are not near. It helps to strengthen that invisible string which connects you, even when you are apart. It's also a really lovely thing to do and brings on feelings of fuzzy warmth.

'Let me help you with that...'

This is a more therapeutic response than 'For goodness sake, just tidy your room' and will usually get better results. The same applies to putting on shoes, packing a school bag and brushing hair. I'm not saying that we always step in and do everything for them; I'm just saying that we offer help when it's needed. I find that our children often do better at a task when we are nearby. It helps to remember that they may be functioning at a far lower age than we sometimes expect them to be. Ask yourself, 'Would I expect a toddler to be able to do that?' The answer I find, more often than not, is 'no'.

Unconditional treats

What a tedious and horrible world it would be if all the good times had to be earned. I'm a big fan of unconditional treats, whether they are a trip out or some lovely food. We need to help our children to build up experiences of the good times and not reinforce their perceptions of themselves as failures. If they enjoy going to gymnastics every week, then I've found it is best not to link that to having to be good all week in order 'win' the right to go (plus we might need the break too).

You look nice today

It takes few seconds to say, but communicates so much more, including 'I've noticed you' and 'I've experienced you in a positive way.'

Making flexible plans

Like those sand-filled escape routes that run alongside steep, downhill roads, our plans need a means of escape so that we don't all feel locked into some hideous nightmare of a day that was meant to be fun. 'Perhaps we'll go later' or 'I can see that you are going to find this difficult so we'll do something at home instead' are useful phrases. Sometimes it's best just to turn up somewhere late or not at all rather than have raging tears or screaming (or both).

Natural consequences

Natural consequences are about cause and effect in their purest sense. If you don't wear a coat and it's raining, you will get wet, is an example which comes immediately to my mind (I have no idea why). Similarly, if one goes outside in the snow and it's well below zero, one might feel a little cold (another familiar example chez moi). At the more extreme end we may need to explore what would happen should we decide not to put on shoes, or trousers. I wouldn't try this with young children, but as they get older, old enough to own 'tech' and go out into town with their friends, there may come a time when instead of rowing for a hour about the wearing of shorts in mid-winter, it's best just to shrug and say, 'You can choose to wear them, I'm not going to stop you.' I use natural consequences a lot, and if I'm not too jarred off I'll try to assist my child in developing 'predictive thinking'. I might say:

> 'What do you think will happen if you don't do that piece of homework?'

I might (probably won't) get anywhere, but sometimes I do and it's a mini-breakthrough. As children get to the stage where they can look us in the eye, we have to get braver in our use of natural consequences, and sometimes we have to be there to catch them with all the empathy we can muster when they fail.

Managed failure

This is similar to a natural consequence, but is more tightly managed and more useful for the stubborn, spiralling tween. I don't use it very often and only when I am desperate. It will follow weeks and weeks of feeling as though I am preventing failure by taking lots of abuse and tip-toeing around my child as though I am some kind of doormat who is singularly responsible for everyone's state of mind. I always warn in advance. The scenario might be something like this:

> Behaviour has been deteriorating for a while with lots of rudeness and obstructive behaviours. Tempers are running high. Nothing appears to be working. Mr D. and stubborn tween are planning to visit friends the following Saturday morning for a couple of hours. Tween is very excited about going (in between being rude and obstructive). The day before the outing I say, 'Dad is leaving at ten o'clock tomorrow and he really wants you to go with him so let's make sure you are ready on time or what might happen?' We will talk through what might happen. The following day, child is rude and obstructive, very rude in fact. At ten o'clock Dad says he is going to sit in the car and will wait ten minutes for child to finish getting ready and join him. Child sits on floor. Dad comes back at ten minutes past ten and says, 'You found it hard to be ready on time and so I am leaving now.' Child remains on the floor. He leaves. As the car pulls away child will beg for you to take them, promises to be the best child ever ('you are

already the best child ever'), will then tell you that you are horrible and mean and worse and will then throw things at your head. You must stick to your guns and remain emotionally regulated and empathetic (you will be because this has kind of been planned).

In our house a managed failure often ends with long and painful discussion about the past and a big shift. It's like someone changed the music. It also means that Mum and Dad mean what they say, which is a good thing.

I have to stress that this technique is not something I have come across anywhere else. It came about because it felt like it's what we needed to do. It is always carried out with maximum empathy. It is not a punishment.

Pick your battles

This is a really obvious strategy but really difficult to stick to. If you find yourself bringing everyone down in a spiral of negativity (nagging), then step back, walk around the garden and resolve to keep your mouth shut for a bit. If we raise the temperature when a wet towel is left on the bedroom floor, or when someone has given themselves a haircut, there will be nowhere left to go when something much more serious happens. Our moaning and complaining will become background music which everyone will have long ago stopped listening to.

There is also the small issue of shame again. Continual picking and criticising is great fertiliser for shame (and anger).

How many out of ten?

When our children are locked in a cycle of fear and anger and our families are buckling under the stress, I have found this technique can help to unlock the underlying fear and allow a certain amount of sharing to take place. It means being brave and taking a punt:

'I wonder if this anger isn't really about the crumb floating in your juice, but about something bigger than that?'

(Silence.)

'It feels to me like it's something bigger.'

(Silence.)

'Normally you're very calm about things like crumbs in juice.'

'Mmmm' (barely perceptible).

'I wonder if you could help me understand what the big anger is about?'

'No.'

'I can understand that it is very difficult to share.'

'Mmmm.'

'How about then if I guess and you tell me how close I am out of ten?'

'Mmmm.'

'Let me think' (dramatic pause, looking around room), 'is it that your teddy has the wrong jumper on?' (start with something silly).

'No, stupid, zero out of ten.'

'Um, you don't like the biscuit I gave you?'

'Ah no, dah, zero.'

'You were secretly hoping for a Bourbon? I know I was.'

'Focus Mum' (because he really wants me to get it).

'I wonder if it's about feeling angry and scared about what happened to you when you were younger and how it makes you feel different.'

'Ten.'

'And I wonder if you worry that Dad and me are going to give up on you.'

'Eleven.'

This is a real example and led to many fruitful and honest conversations and tears. It felt like the magic key which opened the door which had been locked for a very long time. This technique doesn't always work in our family, but when it does, it really does.

Draw me a picture

Talking can sometimes be too intimate a form of communication for our children. I have learnt just as much about how they are feeling from their notes and drawings and their text messages and emails. As I write I have a sticky-note on my laptop saying, 'Everyone loves you, especially ME! ☺.'

Sometimes the notes will communicate something more difficult like, 'It makes me feel scared when you shout.' I will respond by replying to the note, 'I am so, so sorry that I shouted, I know it makes you feel scared and I don't want that. Thank you for telling me.' There will always be drawings. One showed me with a gust of wind coming out of my mouth and a bright red face. Not one of my finest moments.

'Draw me a picture which shows me how you feel' is where I start.

What sort of parent would I be if...?

I sometimes use this to unlock a stalemate situation. It goes something like this:

'I WISH you'd stop making me eat breakfast' (said with attitude).

'What sort of mother would I be if I didn't give you breakfast in the morning?'

(Pause and no further argument, occasionally 'good point'.)

Our two children now model this with each other and say things like, 'Mum is doing this for your own good' and 'Mum is caring for you, not like some mums of children I know.' This technique shouldn't be over-used.

What happens at school, stays at school

How tempting it can be to dish out our frustration when our child has had a bad day at school. 'Not another detention, what did you do this time?' is not as helpful though as 'Oh dear, that sounds like a difficult day; tell me about it.' Home needs to be a place of welcome and sanctuary from the cruel world outside the front door. I don't mean that we take their side against others, I mean that we offer empathy and catch them when they fall. We also need to remember that we might not (probably aren't) getting the full story. If something serious has gone down at school, then try to wait until you have spoken to a member of staff before committing to a position at home. Even when they've really done something wrong, I have learnt it is best to never, ever 'double punish', that is, dish out a consequence at home for something which has already been dealt with at school. This is a sure way of discouraging honest and open communication, which is the life-blood of our relationships with our children.

Keep one step ahead

As adoptive parents we get pretty talented at predicting which events are likely to yank the pin out of the hand grenade. Whether it's a school trip, a birthday party, an anniversary, think ahead and communicate. If, for example, Mother's Day is always the worst day of the year, remember what made it terrible last year, talk to the children about what they think would make it easier and put your new plan into action (with a back pocket Plan B if necessary). That moment, when you voice a worry that's been worming its way round your child's mind, is a magic connection. It says to your child, 'I get you.' Repeated magic connections like these encourage our children to share their fears and worries with us, instead of bearing them alone. I can't remember who said, 'What's shareable is bearable,' but whoever it was, was spot on.

Triggers

'We don't seem to see the effect of triggers' I thought to myself not days before our son came home and said, 'I hate my new science teacher, he stands too close over me and I don't like his voice and I don't like his smell, he scares me a bit.' No prizes for guessing who he looked an awful lot like. Poor science teacher.

These days I'm much more aware of triggers and am trying to help our children to understand what triggers them and why (and that it is not the science teacher's fault that he looks and smells like a child abuser). I've become particularly aware of 'trauma anniversaries'. The theory goes that if a child was hurt and then placed into foster care just as, say, spring was emerging then the smell of warmth on the soil, that first burst of warm sun on the face may cause deeply buried feelings, emotions and memories to surface. As the years go on, I notice a clearer cyclical nature to the behaviours in our house.

I don't know of any magic solutions which take away or significantly reduce the impact of triggers other than the usual therapeutic approaches. Sometimes just being aware of triggers can unlock the empathy and insight we need to help our children to understand and to make better sense of things.

Bonfire of the burdens

Without any prompting from me our son asked if he could write down some things he wanted to be freed from and then burn them. I've no idea what he wrote on his little scraps of paper, but we held a short ceremony in the garden and toasted the flames with mugs of hot chocolate. He seemed unburdened as a result and he's repeated the process since. I've learnt that the most I can do is to facilitate and support these types of events.

Warning: Mum's tired

'My pint glass is empty' is my way of communicating that being crashed around by the waves of trauma has done me in for the day. I (mostly) wake up with my pint glass full. Each drama, each fight, each missile drains the pint glass, until there is nothing but a few drops left. 'You might want to keep out of my way' means that my face might turn red and a hot wind might come from my mouth if I am called upon to deal with any more dramas. Sometimes I need to add, 'I'll be back to normal tomorrow' (at which there will be sniggers at how 'not normal' I am even on a good day).

That makes me feel…

'That makes me sad/angry/disappointed/hurt.*' (*Delete or add as appropriate.)

It is important I think to teach our children that we have feelings and that their behaviour can impact upon our feelings. I don't think it's right to bounce back with a skip and a jump right after having been called a 'b***h' or some such other wounding insult. This is not about shame; it is about communication and learning that our actions impact upon others.

Withdrawing

If a child wants a fight with me and is raising the stakes and fuelling the fire and I think I may not be able to maintain control over my emotions, then I walk away, right after I've told them I'm walking away and why. If the drama has been high and the insults hot and sharp, then I may need to withdraw for a few hours. Mr D. will advise everyone that I need some time on my own and that I am feeling sad and hurt. He will not enter the battle but will explain and stay close. Eventually I will return to the fold and there will be a reconciliation. I might say, 'What sort of person would I be if I wasn't affected by what you did and said?' I might talk about how they have felt when treated badly by a friend. I will always reinforce the 'no matter what' message.

This technique is rarely used in our house but has been highly effective at breaking a cycle of anger, aggression and abusiveness by giving time for reflection. It puts us as parents back in the driving seat and removes us from the cycle of receiving abuse, followed by a hollow apology, followed by more abuse, and so on. It is another one of those techniques, which, when used with care, can change the landscape.

Sharing stories of failure

Our children love to hear about the time I nearly wet my pants at school. It was a double maths lesson, with a teacher who wasn't usually ours. She was the scariest woman I have ever come across in my life. She bore a remarkable likeness to the head Dalek from *Dr Who* and for that reason we used to call her Davros. Davros asked me to organise some test papers in some strange and ill-explained way, based on the scores at the top of the papers. I misunderstood, was too scared to ask her to explain again, got it wrong and was showered with a tirade of venom spit from her wrinkled old mouth. She was the stuff of nightmares. This story chimes with our children, I think, because I am sharing my infallibility in a way which rings true for them; that fear of misunderstanding, that weakness, that bladder-emptying terror that an adult can inflict upon a child. It is also about school which is so often the focus of failure for our children.

Mind jumping

'How would that have felt for my child?' is my first port of call when anything of any significance has happened and I predict a fallout. If a best friend is moving school, or a neighbour's dog has died, or the weatherman is forecasting a big thunderstorm, then there is no point me sticking with how I feel about those events. I need to try to get inside my child's head, so I can be there with the empathy and the coping strategies. Our children really like it when you can demonstrate you can do this and it means they don't have to tell us by throwing shoes at us.

Feeling out loud

Without warning and out of the blue I might say, 'Today I feel unsettled and I don't know why,' or 'I feel marvellously happy and I wonder why.' I will be reporting on my genuine feelings and being curious about them. I stumbled upon this technique because I used it naturally and two little lights came on. That's a sign in our house that we're on to something useful.

It was wrong but I get why

'It was wrong for you to take the money, but I get why you wanted it' is better than 'For the love of mother earth why EVER did you TAKE THE MONEY!' In order to help our children to change their behaviours, we need to understand them first.

Shock tactics

'After a particularly terrible day full of bad behaviour, why not reward them with a small treat?' is something you would never hear from the parenting experts. Well, I use this tactic and I like it. If we've had a difficult few days and a child has gone off to school vexing about what a witch I've been, they will most likely have spent the day dreading the return home. They will not only dread it, but may pump themselves up ready for another confrontation. The tactical shock treat takes the wind out of the sails of pumped-up confrontation. So, too, can the shock text, 'You hurt me with what you said. I don't think you meant it. See you later. Love Mum xx.'

Come and sit with me

You know those times when a child finds it hard to open their mouths without a stream of rudeness pouring out? And no matter how, 'Don't speak to me like that' you get, it just makes it worse? When 'SORREEE' gets thrown at you right before 'IDIOT'? When you can no longer touch the bottom with your toes and risk drowning in a vile sea of rudeness? It's those times when I most itch to resort to traditional parenting-type and sometimes do (right before regretting it). But there doesn't seem to be much in the therapeutic parenting toolbox for times like these (don't send them to another room, don't shout, don't threaten, don't take things away) and we can be left taking it like some pathetic flake of a person.

This is what I do:

'That was very rude and if you speak to Dad like that again you will leave the table' (it's a mealtime, of course!).

'OH MY GOD, I can't STAND you, IDIOT' (because the warning never ever, ever works).

'Come and sit with me' (and we sit together somewhere near the kitchen table, yet removed from it) and everyone else carries on.

There will be complaining and moaning and more rudeness, but it eventually subsides. Maybe we'll have to repeat the process (we will for sure) but it is the only way I've found of (a) not being a shouty nag witch; (b) not overheating; or (c) ignoring it until it becomes 'normal'. In the interests of honesty I must just point out that sometimes Mr D. and I will have had enough and one of us may just leave the table and eat elsewhere. Or we may shout untherapeutically. Or both.

Filling their toolbox

As our children have got older it's become more obvious to me that they need to be helped to develop tools which will help them to navigate their way through life (I mentioned this in Chapter 9, 'Life Story Work'). Although their trauma symptoms are reducing over time, they are not likely to go away altogether. Helping them to understand what hyper-vigilance is and why they have it has helped them to feel less 'crazy'. Teaching them how to avoid crowded places, how to walk down the street without being distracted, ways of burning off the stressy 'fizz' they sometimes come home from school with, how to think ahead and predict natural consequences are all skills which will stand them in good stead for the future. Talking with adults who have experienced trauma has helped me to see that these sorts of coping strategies give children and young people a foundation to work from.

Celebrate the wins

Slowly, but surely, progress will be made. It may at times feel so slow that you hardly notice it. But if you really think about it, or if you look back at photographs or a diary, then you might be struck by how far you've come. Perhaps one day the PE bag will come home and nothing will be missing, or you'll find a note on your pillow that says 'I love you very much,' or you'll overhear something of such depth and intelligence it will blow you away. Many of our children can't cope with praise, so we can't make a big deal of their successes. Sometimes in our family we demonstrate praise, rather then speak it: something extra lovely for tea, with fizzy drinks in special glasses to make a toast to the good times. So whatever stage you're at in the hilly marathon that is adoptive parenting, look out for me when you get to the top, and we'll appreciate the view because it's going to be amazing.